Community Policing:
A Handbook for Beat Cops and Supervisors

by

Lieutenant Howard Rahtz
Cincinnati Police Department

Criminal Justice Press
Monsey, New York

2001

This book is dedicated to the men and women of the Cincinnati Police Division, who perform with courage and compassion under sometimes trying circumstances.

Printed in the United States of America. No part of this book may be reproduced in any manner whatsoever without written permission, except for brief quotations embodied in critical articles and reviews. For information, contact Criminal Justice Press, Willow Tree Press Inc., P.O. Box 249, Monsey, NY 10952 U.S.A.

ISBN: 1-881798-29-1 (paper)

Contents

ACKNOWLEDGMENTS

Thanks to John Eck who taught me a lot about problem solving; to Phyllis Caskey who encouraged me to try things out; to the staff at the Cincinnati Police Academy who personify excellence; and to Kathy, Denny, Christine, and Caroline — without you guys none of the rest of it matters.

ABOUT THE AUTHOR

Howard Rahtz is a lieutenant with the Cincinnati Police Division. He is currently assigned to the Police Academy. He previously served as a beat officer, patrol supervisor, supervisor in the Police Division's Community Oriented Policing Program, Assistant Director of the Planning and Research Section, and shift commander.

In 1997, he received the Hamilton County (Ohio) Police Association Award for Contributions to Law Enforcement. He is an adjunct faculty member at the University of Cincinnati, and a trainer for the Tri-State Regional Community Policing Institute. He lives in Cincinnati with his wife and three children.

Foreword

It is refreshing to see a book that gets right to the purpose of Community Policing. During my career as a police officer, supervisor, administrator, and university professor, I have witnessed many attempts by law enforcement professionals and academics to explain and/or define community policing. Most of them missed the target. The written literature, which is regularly increasing, deals mostly with versions of how community policing differs from the traditional model. Much is written to help provide background and learning material for college students in criminal justice programs. Books utilized for police promotional exams usually deal with definitions, and focus on what is *not* considered community-oriented policing.

Seldom is found a straightforward explanation of Community-Oriented Policing, and even more rare is a specific handbook designed for the beat cop and his supervisors. Lieutenant Rahtz calls on his expertise as a former beat cop and supervisor in the Cincinnati Police Division, a community-policing agency. He cites real-life examples of community policing, emphasizing the "results-oriented" approach.

The theme of "Community Partnerships" reso-
nates throughout the book. The examples are from
around the country and involve real officers working in
real neighborhoods. Most police officers will easily
identify with many of the problems presented. More
importantly, they should benefit from the novel and
creative approaches outlined by the officers working
on the problems.

Lieutenant Rahtz points out that "Problem Solving" is at the heart of many of these "Community Partnerships." The importance of the problem-solving process is explained. Excellent examples are utilized in
which beat officers and their supervisors, in any jurisdiction, will learn new methods and techniques that
may be modified for their use locally.

Finally, Lieutenant Rahtz outlines some practical
advice on exactly how the beat cop can get started
when assigned to a new territory. He provides step-by-
step guidelines, which should be very helpful to any
officer interested in working as part of the Community
Policing.

Keep in mind the importance of the supervisory
role in facilitating a successful community polic-
ing/problem-solving mode. The support and direction
of these supervisors will determine the effectiveness of
community policing in any police agency.

True, there are a number of other ingredients necessary for a police agency to maintain itself as a high-quality community-policing organization. For example, training, both at the front door (new officer) and ongoing (in-service) throughout the year, ensures that the most current skills and techniques are not only made available to the officer but are reinforced.

I think this book goes to the heart of what it takes to be a successful officer or supervisor in community policing. Careful attention in explaining details of the many examples, as well as a specific step-by-step process to assist in problem solving, makes this book a valuable resource in training programs. The easy-to-read format and straightforward approach, combined with the authentic examples, make this book a "must read" for the serious practitioner.

Lieutenant Colonel Ted J. Schoch (Ret.)
Cincinnati Police Academy Director

Chapter 1.
Community-Oriented
Policing (COP)

Community-Oriented Policing (COP) — a lot of beat cops cringe at the phrase. COP, often shortened to "community policing," conjures up images of cops playing basketball with kids, walking a beat in an "officer-friendly" manner, going to neighborhood meetings to be grilled by irate citizens, and a lot of other things that don't look much like real police work.

In some places these images of community policing are all too accurate. Somebody writes a grant or comes back from a conference, and all of a sudden the powers that be are hot to do community policing. The department grabs the grant, sets up a few days of training on the "Community Policing Model," a few cops are designated community officers, the chief holds a press conference, and nothing really changes. Too often, for the guy on the beat, COP is just one more specialized unit that means fewer people to do the day-to-day grunt work of answering the radio.

COP has much to offer, but it suffers from its history. It's a model of policing that flies in the face of what most of us have learned about police work. A lot of the background of COP comes from academia, where it's easy to sit in a classroom and pontificate about what police ought to do. But most of all, because of the way it has been presented, COP seems like a program with no real benefits for the cop on the street.

This book takes a different tack. Community policing, for those cops willing to give it a try, means being a more effective beat officer. It takes officers out of that professional stance in which they tell an elderly woman afraid on her own street — "Keep your doors locked and call 911 when something happens." Or to the business owner being forced out of the community by disorderly teens gathering in front of his business — "I can't do anything about it. It's not against the law to stand on the corner." Or, "I can't talk now, I've got a radio run to make."

Real community policing is intelligent policing grounded in what most cops pride themselves on — common sense. It means getting off the treadmill of chasing the radio and making after-the-fact reports. It means standing up for the elderly woman imprisoned by fear in her own home. It means standing up for the business people and citizens who are bullied and intimidated by the thugs in the community. It's for cops who understand that if we're going to turn the situation in our neighborhoods around, it's not going to be done by police administrators writing grand reports, detectives handling crime scenes, or community relations officers going to neighborhood meetings. It's going to be done by street cops taking some pride in their beat and believing they can make a difference.

WHAT WE'RE DOING ISN'T WORKING

For most beat officers, the 911 system is the primary determinant of their daily activity. They respond to radio runs on their beats, take reports, call in specialized units (investigators, gang officers, etc.) when necessary, and devote any remaining time to random patrol. Under this traditional model of policing, police presence, prowling the community in a patrol car, is a deterrent to would-be crooks. If any criminal should be bold enough to commit a crime, officers quickly respond, nabbing the crook at the scene. If our bad guy manages to get away, detectives arrive to process the crime scene and, through the wonders of forensic science, nail the unknown perpetrator.

– 3 –

As every rookie cop quickly learns, it just doesn't work that way. She responds "lights and sirens" to a robbery, only to meet a victim who informs her the offense occurred 20 minutes earlier.

"Why didn't you call right away?" our irritated rookie asks.

Our victim looks at the cop in disbelief. "I had to call my mama," he retorts.

In fact, research on rapid response bears out our rookie's experience. A 1970s study in Kansas City found rapid response led to an arrest in only 3% of serious crimes (Kelling et al., 1975). Later studies in Jacksonville, Peoria, Rochester, and San Diego all found similar results (Kelling and Stewart, 1991).

Most people delay between 20 and 40 minutes before calling the police. Some are in shock. Some are worried that the criminal is still close by, and they want to make sure he is really gone. For a lot of victims, the first reaction is to go someplace where they feel safe, and then, after thinking it over, they may or may not call the police. Moreover, many victims *never* call the police because they either think it won't do any good or they are afraid of retaliation.

After completing paperwork on the robbery, our rookie is back on patrol. She is hoping to come across a crime in progress and lock up a bad guy. But the odds are against her. The majority of crimes, about two-thirds, are committed outside the public view. Those that occur on the street happen quickly. The average street robbery lasts about 90 seconds (Bieck et al., 1991). Consider the geographic area that constitutes a police beat, and then calculate the odds of being in a certain location in a minute and a half time frame. Our rookie may go her whole career without happening on a crime in progress.

But what about the deterrent effect? Just patrolling the streets creates a sense of police omnipresence that prevents crime. That's what our rookie was likely told at the police academy. Again, the facts speak otherwise. The famous Kansas City Random Patrol experiment found no differences in reported crime between beats heavy with patrol cars and those beats where police responded only when called (Kelling et al., 1975).

The one place where our rookie can have some impact is during the initial investigation of reported crimes. The TV image shows the beat cop guarding the perimeter, waiting for the "suits" from the detective bureau to show up and solve the crime. Again, reality is otherwise. The biggest single factor in solving crimes is the quality of preliminary investigations carried out by the first responding officers (Bieck et al., 1991). Effort, in that first few minutes, put into locating witnesses and gathering information from people at the scene has more of a payoff than all the scientific analysis that TV cops rely on.

Under the traditional model of policing, success is measured by response time, arrests made, and a high investigative case closure rate. The pressure on the beat cop is to get there fast, handle it, and get back on the air.

As a patrol supervisor, I answered a lot of complaints about slow response time. And pity the cop who is "laying off the air," keeping himself out of service. It's interesting that the most important part of the process, what the officer actually does on the scene, receives the least attention. As long as he gets there fast, handles the problem quickly, and gets back on the air, the officer is deemed to have done a good job.

THE TYRANNY OF THE RADIO

Think for a second about the purpose of police agencies. Forget the noble-sounding mission statements that adorn the walls of police stations all over the country. Instead concentrate on what citizens expect of police and what police officers believe their job to be. In truth, the mission in most agencies has become "answer the radio."

In fact, "answering the radio" is not the mission of the police, but simply one tool to accomplish our basic mission. And what is that mission? Sir Robert Peel, considered the father of modern policing, described the business of policing as *keeping the peace* and *preventing crime*. We might phrase it differently today, but it would be hard to find a police executive who wouldn't consider including those two phrases in his own agency's mission statement. The point is that responding to radio runs is a means to accomplish the mission, not the mission itself.

Responding to radio runs has come to be almost synonymous with providing police service. It is what police officers do. The myth of rapid response and the success in selling 911 policing to the public have probably been the biggest factors in creating demand for police services, but societal changes have contributed as well.

Two or three times in an eight-hour tour, most cops walk away from a situation in utter amazement at how absolutely inept people are at solving their own problems. Police officers respond to a "family trouble" call in which a mother dialed 911 because her nine-year-old son won't do his homework; or two teen siblings got in a fight, and the parents called wanting one or both arrested for domestic violence.

In most families, parents, aunts and uncles, or other family members intervene and mediate these disputes. Effectively handling family problems is one of the major functions of parents. With the well-documented breakdown in families, the number of children basically raising themselves has increased dramatically, leaving cops to respond more and more as surrogate mother and father.

RESPONDING TO THE FAILURES OF OTHER COMMUNITY INSTITUTIONS

The breakdown of other community institutions has also contributed to the beat cop's workload. Schools and mental health institutions are two examples. In schools, violence and drug dealing are an all-too-familiar part of the educational experience for many children. Security staff, police officers, and metal detectors have become as much a part of the school landscape as cheerleaders and marching bands.

The problems afflicting schools are complex, but the bottom line for police officers is that as schools have deteriorated police officers are forced to spend more time in schools responding to assaults, breaking up fights, and dealing with complaints of drugs and weapons.

Changes in the mental health system have had an enormous impact on police. As patients have been shifted in large numbers from institutions to community-based care, some have fallen through cracks (more accurately, crevices) in the system. Beat cops most often meet them as victims of street predators, who see these individuals as fair game for assault and robbery.

All too often — due to lack of medical supervision, problems with medication, or other reasons — mentally ill people trigger calls to the police. These "mental" dispatches run the gamut from a request to transport the patient to the hospital (using police as an expensive taxi service) to handling an out-of-control violent individual. In essence, every one of these dispatches represents a failure of the mental health system that becomes a police problem.

GETTING OFF THE TREADMILL

To a rookie cop, answering the radio is exciting, and she speeds from run to run, giving a lecture to an unruly kid, scattering a group of teens on the corner, mediating a family fight, taking a theft report. She handles each situation as quickly as possible, gets back on the air, and cruises the beat waiting for the next dispatch. As time goes by, our rookie begins to notice that a lot of her runs are repetitive. She gets a dispatch for disorderly persons and realizes this is the same address where she was sent last week for loud music, the week before that for family trouble, the week before that for an assault. But, typically, the rookie treats each one as a separate incident. She advises, sends someone on his or her way, lectures or makes an arrest and the situation is resolved — for that day.

But the next day, or a week later, or a month later, the rookie will be making another radio run to that same location, dealing with the same offenders and the same victims. In fact, research shows that over 60% of radio runs are made to 10% of addresses; 10% of offenders commit 55% of crimes; and 10% of victims are involved in 40% of crimes (Bieck et al., 1991).

The police respond, dealing with each incident, never truly solving the underlying problem. Officers soon get to feeling like a hamster on a treadmill, dealing with similar situations and the same people over and over again.

There is a more intelligent way, and that's Community-Oriented Policing.

Chapter 2.
Community Policing:
Dueling Definitions

COMMUNITY POLICE AND THE "REAL" POLICE

"You better take good care of them boys," the sheriff said. "Cause if you don't, they'll kill any program you come up with." The sheriff was a panel member making a presentation on COP for some criminal justice students. He described community policing as "effective PR," and was warning students about the media, specifically their ability to sway public opinion for or against the police.

The next speaker, a university professor, took a more academic bent. He emphasized the long history of community policing, talking about "The Quiet Revolution," early foot patrol experiments, and "broken windows."

The last speaker, a chief in a mid-sized town, talked up his department's bike patrol, the Drug Abuse Resistance Education (DARE) program they had in area schools, and the block watch program he had recently started in a crime-ridden neighborhood.

I walked out behind a couple of uniformed cops who'd been in attendance. "What did you think?" one asked his partner. In response, the cop yanked his handcuffs out from his belt. "Here's my COP program," he said. "I don't know a whole lot about 'broken windows,' but I am pretty good at arresting assholes."

They laughed and so did I. But who was right? Is the beat cop who's out there "cuffing and stuffing" doing COP? Or is it only those officers riding bikes or working in schools? And what do "broken windows" have to do with anything?

The issue is a hot one, not only in academic circles, but in station houses as well. In *Issues in Community Policing* (Dukes and Kratcoski, 1995), a collection of works by criminal justice researchers, nearly every article begins with that particular author's definition of community policing. Is it just the old community relations effort in a new dress? Is it foot patrol?

Is it problem solving on the beat? Are the cops supposed to be social workers? Do they still make arrests?

The debate in precincts and station houses around the country is less polite. Officers in the COPE program, the community police effort in Baltimore County (Maryland), were referred to by the beat officers as "Cops on Pension Early." In Houston, the Neighborhood-Oriented Policing program (NOP) was ridiculed as "Nobody on Patrol" (Goldstein, 1990). The "Love Police" was a common phrase heard in discussions of COP in Cincinnati.

The hostility a lot of beat cops feel toward community policing is not difficult to understand. To many beat cops, COP is just one more specialized unit, leaving more and more real police work (making radio runs) to fewer and fewer patrol officers. Add in the perks that many COP officers enjoy (flexible hours, offices and desks, weekends off) and such resentment is natural. In addition, COP in many agencies is so poorly structured and managed that it is an easy target for ridicule.

To the beat guy drowning in radio runs, taking cops off the street to work with kids or to focus on neighborhood problems seems the height of bureaucratic lunacy. The old saying that goes, "When you're up to your ass in alligators, it's hard to remember your objective is draining the swamp," seems particularly fitting. And police managers have done a poor job connecting Community-Oriented Policing to the day-to-day work of beat cops.

"BROKEN WINDOWS"

In 1982, James Wilson and George Kelling wrote an article for the *Atlantic Monthly* entitled "Broken Windows." Both Wilson and Kelling were well-respected criminal justice researchers, and their article would mark the beginning of important changes in the way police managers and officers alike viewed policing.

Wilson and Kelling made the common sense connection between "community disorder" and crime. If a window in a building is broken and left unrepaired, pretty soon all the windows in that building will be broken. When property is abandoned or weeds and litter are allowed to accumulate on a vacant lot, soon a junk auto or two appear on the scene. Graffiti appear on the side of a building, and a few days later the building is covered with it. Then, the graffiti spread to other properties.

Groups of young men gather on corners, harassing and intimidating passers-by. Business owners complain that their customers are afraid to come in the store. The groups on the corner begin to openly drink alcohol, use and sell drugs. The corner becomes a site of frequent fights, robberies, and even drive-by shootings. Residents who have the resources move to other neighborhoods. Owner-occupied housing is replaced by rental property, which is often occupied by people who have little stake or interest in the community. As businesses leave, the deterioration spreads like a cancer. Boarded up buildings, covered with graffiti, become the backdrop for groups of young men roaming the streets intimidating and victimizing the good citizens still left in the neighborhood.

Every experienced cop has seen this happen in one neighborhood or another. It sometimes happens slowly, over a period of years. At other times, a neighborhood can, as a friend of mine observed, "go to shit in a big hurry."

As crime and disorder take over the neighborhood, beat cops end up speeding from one call to the next, taking reports, making arrests, and accomplishing almost nothing.

The problem is that under the traditional or reactive policing model, these "community disorder" problems are not really police problems. Litter, overgrown lots — call Sanitation! An abandoned building — not our problem! Kids loitering on the corner — if they're not breaking the law, there's nothing we can do about it! Call us when something happens.

The good news is that community policing efforts in a lot of cities have proven that attention to these disorder problems will have an impact on crime rates. Fixing these community "broken windows" will lead to less crime and disorder and an improved quality of life not only for citizens in the neighborhood, but for the beat cops working there as well.

COP: WHAT IT IS AND WHAT IT'S NOT...

Let's look at a couple of beat cops as they go about their jobs. They work similar beats, similar populations. But they have decidedly different approaches to police work.

Officer Jack represents the traditional policing mold. After roll call, he heads out to his patrol car, puts on his sunglasses, turns the air conditioner on high, winds up the windows, and hits the street. Right out of the box, he gets a "neighbor trouble" run. "God damn it," he thinks, "I was there last week." Jack pulls up to the scene, and separates the participants. As the parties compete to give Jack their side of the story, he cuts them off with a stern wave.

"I'm not here to referee your stupid arguments," he tells them. "All I know is if I come back here to-night, both of you are going to jail." He orders them inside their houses and puts himself back on the air. Ten minutes from start to finish. That should keep the bosses happy.

Half a coffee later, he gets another run. Mr. Anonymous, calling again about disorderly teens on the corner at Benson and Hedges. Jack pulls up, gives them "the stare," and they begin to move slowly around the corner. "Sent on way," Jack tells the dis-patcher and heads for his hole (a nice quiet spot behind a school) to finish his coffee in peace.

A while later, it's an alarm run. Jack recognizes the address. It's that old lady again — always screwing up the alarm system and creating paperwork. Jack dis-regards his backup. Mrs. O'Riley is at the door when Jack pulls up.

"Oh, dear. Did I set it off again?" she asks.

Jack fills in the paper and tells her to lock the door. Jack's in a hurry. Mr. Anonymous is calling again. This time, one of the kids on the corner, the one in the green shirt, has a gun.

Jack pulls up and jumps out of the car, gun in hand. He orders the kids to "prone out" on the ground. He checks green shirt first. No gun. Same old story. He quickly checks the others and finding nothing, sends them on their way, threatening to arrest them if he sees them back on the corner tonight. Jack heads back to his car, fantasizing about choking Mr. Anonymous.

Jack is on his way to well-deserved dinner when the radio dispatcher calls him again — trouble at the Dew Drop Inn, a couple of drunken customers in a fight. Fortunately, by the time Jack arrives, everyone is friends again. The bartender sticks his head out the door and gives Jack the OK sign. Finally a break! He doesn't even have to get out of the car.

After dinner, Jack pulls into his favorite "fishing hole," a lightly traveled intersection where Jack can easily get some stop-sign violators. It's the end of the month and Jack needs a few traffic tickets to keep the bosses happy. In an hour, he's got four tickets on people who rolled through the stop sign — a good night's work. Jack fills out his worksheet, gets his paperwork in order, and heads into the station.

Officer Pete goes about his job in a little different fashion. Prior to roll call, he catches the officer working Pete's beat on the previous shift, checking to see if anything significant occurred. Pete checks the crime board for offenses on his beat in the past 24 hours, then glances through the auto accident reports, mentally noting the locations.

After roll call, Pete meets with the detective assigned to his beat. There are no real suspects in a recent street robbery and nothing to go on but a nickname, "Peanut," provided by a witness.

Pete gets his coffee and heads to a large apartment building that is one of the trouble spots on his beat. Pete is sitting together with the owner during an interview with a prospective tenant. The presence of a uniformed police officer has been an excellent screening device, and over the past six months the building has shown real improvement. Pete is getting fewer and fewer runs to that address.

After the interview, Pete spots a group of kids standing on a corner where residents have complained of abusive and disorderly teens. He gets out to talk to them, noticing that one of them is a kid he hasn't seen before. After some small talk, Pete gets enough information on the kid — name, address, birth date, school, etc. — to make a Field Interrogation Report (FIR) card. Pete notices a gang tattoo on the kid's left forearm and notes it on the FIR card. Pete sends the kids on their way, warning them not to hang on the corner. After the kids leave, Pete goes into the corner grocer across the street for some conversation with the owner.

"I haven't seen the kid with the tattoo before," Pete says. "Do you know anything about him?"

"Kind of a hard kid," the shopkeeper tells Pete. "Lives a block over with his mother. I had problems with him the other day."

"If you hear anything else about him, let me know," Pete says, and heads back to his car.

Between radio runs, Pete decides to check the intersection where an auto accident happened on his day off. The problem is obvious. A bush has grown too large, obscuring the view. Pete makes a note to call his contact at Highway Maintenance to get the bush trimmed.

As Pete is heading for the station at the end of his shift, the shopkeeper pages him. "I just remembered something about that kid," he says. "It's probably not important, but the other kids keep calling him 'Peanut.'"

COP IS A PHILOSOPHY... AND A WAY OF DOING BUSINESS

In our little scenarios above, which cop would you want on the beat in your neighborhood? If your family needed the police, whom would you rather have respond?

Community policing is a philosophy, but it's a philosophy of action. And it's night and day different from the incident-driven 911 policing that most of us learned as young officers.

A lot of cops get hung up on this point when COP is described, as it typically is, as an organizational philosophy. "If it's an organizational philosophy, then it's a management thing. I'm not involved." Or, as I often hear in training — "What you're saying makes a lot of sense. The Chief should hear this."

The attitude seems to be that COP is something only an organization does, not the individual. It is true that as individual officers much of what we do is organizationally defined. But it is also true that even in the most rigid, micro-managed agencies, individual officers are able to develop their own style of policing that can be as different as Jack and Pete's.

When we pin on that badge, we don't turn off our brains. One of the truly distinctive things about police work is the tremendous discretion that individual officers enjoy. Despite some police managers' attempts to control every aspect of officer behavior, every cop goes about his work in a very individualistic fashion. How we talk to people, the way we carry ourselves, the thoroughness with which we investigate, the demeanor we put on for crooks and good citizens — these are all things that no procedure manual or supervisor can truly control.

The point is that while COP is a philosophy, it's one that can be individually applied. When I was a beat cop, there was an apartment building where residents frequently reported thefts from autos. I completed about 10 reports there before it sank in that I could do more than just make the paper. I contacted the apartment owner and explained the problem. He upgraded the lighting in the parking lot, ending the string of thefts from cars that were plaguing the tenants. He also saved me and the other cops assigned there some serious paperwork. That's COP in action, and in hindsight I wonder why it took me so long.

Like Pete, if an officer takes that COP attitude on every run, the day-to-day problems that beat cops struggle with begin to look much different.

A WAY OF DOING BUSINESS... NOT A PROGRAM

To say that COP is "not a program" means that the chief who points to his DARE program as COP is as full of crap as the sheriff who describes his COP program as "just good media relations." Real community policing is not a program that is found on an organizational chart or tacked onto a deputy chief's job description. It is a philosophy that permeates an organization, a way of going about the business of policing that is distinct from the incident-driven policing of the past.

There are a lot of good "programs" that could be part of community policing. Block watch, DARE, citizen police academies — these are all examples of programs that might be constructive pieces of community policing. But these programs, without the COP philosophical underpinning, are simply stand-alone efforts.

A lot of forward-thinking police leaders are taking the distinction between "philosophy" and "program" under COP to its logical conclusion by doing away with designated positions like "COP Officer." The underlying thinking is that if, in fact, COP is a philosophy that is organization-wide, we defeat ourselves by labeling only a few officers as COP specialists, leaving the rest of the organization to go about business as usual.

A WAY OF DOING BUSINESS... NOT A TACTIC

Foot patrol and bike patrol are two police tactics that have been closely associated with community policing. In fact, much of the impetus for community policing sprang from early foot-patrol experiments in Newark, New Jersey, and Flint, Michigan (Kelling and Coles, 1996). Foot patrol and bike patrol are important in community policing because they make officers more accessible to the community and facilitate the process of developing the relationships necessary to solve community problems. But in and of themselves, they are not community policing. A foot patrol officer, walking his area in an aloof and distant fashion, is not much different from the traditional officer who cruises the community in his patrol car, windows up, waiting for a radio run.

Real community policing does not require having all officers out walking the beat eight hours a day. The patrol car is an important tool for effective policing, and it makes no more sense to ignore it than it does to ignore foot patrol as a potentially important patrol tactic.

Community policing mixes and matches tactics to correspond to community problems and concerns. In some instances, foot patrol is appropriate, and in other instances, motor patrol is more effective. Community policing calls for an intelligent application of both.

SOFT ON CRIMINALS?

This is probably the most damning accusation made about COP. After all, locking up bad people is what most of us signed on to do. The problem is that sometimes locking up people is not a terrific way to solve a problem. "Are you saying we shouldn't lock up people who break the law?" No, I'm not saying that at all. Let's use the drug problem in our communities as an example.

As cops in both cities and small towns understand, the movement of drug trafficking into a neighborhood is a disaster, particularly for the people who live there. The police respond. We do buy-busts, we do drug sweeps, we use informants, we get search warrants and we kick in doors. We confiscate huge quantities of drugs, money, cars, and any other property we can seize under asset-forfeiture laws. We call press conferences and pose with weapons, drugs, and money all laid out for the media to admire. When a few brave souls raise the issue of whether we're having any impact, we quote them statistics on the arrests we've made, the kilos of dope confiscated, and the bundles of money seized.

A bust of a major dealer in southwest Ohio illustrates the problem. According to an August 1998 article in the *Cincinnati Enquirer*, a joint operation involving the U.S. Drug Enforcement Administration (DEA) and local police netted a local drug kingpin believed to be a major supplier of drugs in the area. The investigation began with a traffic stop in Nebraska, where a search of the vehicle of a Cincinnati man found over 100 pounds of marijuana. Six months later, the three people running the drug ring were arrested. Commenting on the significance of the arrest, the local prosecutor said, "It's a huge amount of drugs to move." But one of the beat cops questioned put this bust into perspective.

"The DEA did a good job on this," the officer stated. "Don't get me wrong. They got a break on it and I'm glad, but we're still seeing the same level of drugs out there we saw before. You got one (drug dealer) down, you got two to take his place."

This same scenario plays out thousands of times across the country on a daily basis. It's not soft on crime to question the results. Studies from California to New Jersey are showing that problem solving and community-policing efforts are more effective in solving neighborhood drug problems than traditional police tactics have been (Green, 1996).

Arrest is one tool. Sometimes it's the most effective one to use and sometimes it's not. Community policing gives us more tools to use. It doesn't require a rocket scientist to suggest we ought to make use of all of them.

FOCUS ON RESULTS

If we focus on numbers, our traditional police officer Jack will no doubt look like a better officer. He makes a lot of arrests, writes a lot of tickets. The question is — what is he actually accomplishing?

Think about the commonplace problem of "kids on the corner." The typical response is like Jack's. Pull up, give them the "look," and drive off. The kids go around the corner and a few minutes later, they strut back, having a laugh at the officer's expense and frustrating the citizens who expect the police to do something about the problem. What a lot of citizens then do is raise the stakes. Since their perception is the police are not taking their complaint seriously, they call in again. Only this time the complaint is a man with a gun. That generally brings the cops quickly, but creates a potentially lethal confrontation that really could have been prevented.

Even at best, the problems for Officer Jack may multiply. Witnesses complain about excessive force. The boy's family and friends are convinced it's an example of police harassment and brutality in the neighborhood. Internal Affairs may get a complaint, and though Jack is likely to be exonerated the process itself galls him. No one — not the kid, not Jack, not the caller — is happy with the outcome. And no one really understands what happened.

The problem of disorderly kids on the corner is a difficult one for every beat officer confronted with the situation. But new research on "hot-spot policing" is proving what a lot of cops have discovered on their own — that some simple measures taken by uniformed officers can have a big impact on the problem (Koper, 1998).

NOT JUST PUBLIC RELATIONS

Good public relations are important, and police agencies are generally lousy at it. So much of what passes as public or media relations nowadays is the phony baloney nonsense of spin doctors and media consultants. It's no wonder people, especially cops, are skeptical of everything and anything that comes dressed as public relations. Community policing, done correctly, is emphatically not a public relations exercise. Working with people in the community, trying to develop partnerships for problem solving, is hard work. There are going to be ups and downs, some successes, and some stinkers. Community policing is the opposite of slick. It relies on hard work and honesty, something that is not often part of PR campaigns.

Police leaders like the sheriff who believes community policing is just public relations are no different from the political hacks working hard at putting the proper "spin" on everything that happens.

PREVENTION ORIENTATION

Jack writes tickets at times and locations where he knows he can get "an easy bump." Pete sees his job not as writing tickets, but as preventing fatal and injury accidents. If we are called to repeated accidents at the same location, the odds are good that some physical changes, such as improved traffic controls, might help. Good beat cops know more about what changes can improve traffic safety than anyone else. But a lot of cops would say, "That's not our job. Call Traffic Engineering."

A prevention philosophy says, let's look at the underlying causes and then solve the problem. The "not our job" philosophers take accident reports, sit on traffic posts, and make death notifications.

NOT JUST A POLICE RESPONSIBILITY

Community policing says that crime and disorder are not just police problems, but community problems.

And that other groups have an obligation to work together with the police to solve these problems. In the past, police defined themselves as "law enforcement," and crime control was our turf. If crime increased, it just meant we needed more cops. Today, there is increasing recognition that partnerships with community groups of all sorts are an effective way of controlling crime.

So what is community policing? It can be summed up simply — a results-oriented approach to policing that can be both organizationally and individually applied, partnerships to help us accomplish our mission, and a commitment to solving community problems.

Chapter 3.
Partnerships: The Glue of Community Policing

Avondale, a troubled neighborhood in Cincinnati, is just like thousands of others around the country. High crime levels, open-air drug markets, struggling businesses, groups of teens fighting over street corners... every cop knows the picture. And most of them feel powerless to do much about it. It's poverty, teen pregnancy, racism, homelessness, single-parent families, lousy schools, no jobs... The whole laundry list of community woes that social scientists tell us are the causes of crime. The message is that until we do something about all these causes the crime problem will never go away. **They are flat-out wrong**.

Beat cops, working with the people in their neighborhoods, have proven that crime and community disorder can be reduced without waiting for the underlying problems to be solved. I am not saying that poverty, teen pregnancy, etc., are not important issues and do not deserve attention. But if we, as police officers and citizens, sit back in the belief we are impotent in the face of crime until these problems are solved, we are doing a grave disservice to ourselves and our neighborhoods.

A story on Avondale as reported in the February 27, 1999, *Cincinnati Enquirer*, describes the problems faced by the neighborhood:

> Avondale has been one of Cincinnati's most crime-ridden neighborhoods for years... Police say drug-related activities — especially crack cocaine dealing — has been the root of Avondale's problem. Drug dealers attack one another and beat up addicts who don't pay. Cash-strapped users break into cars and homes. Women sell sex for drugs.

What did the beat officers do in this situation? They did what cops typically do. They provided stepped-up enforcement and more arrests. But they also did what beat officer Shawn George called some "little things" to make the bad guys uncomfortable.

They shut down a pay phone that was a central point of loitering and drug dealing. They worked with a business owner to remove some video games from his store because the video games were an attraction that had turned his premises into a gang hangout. They worked with business owners to enforce trespassing laws. They fixed a broken fence that had become an escape route for dealers running from the police.

The key phrase is "worked with." Think about it. How much can we really accomplish as police officers by ourselves? Even our traditional incident-driven cop reacts to what other people do. First, somebody has to report a crime. All of us have experience with uncooperative victims and witnesses. Real successes in policing come from working effectively with other people. The best cops understand and act on this knowledge.

In the Avondale example, officers "fixed a broken fence that had become an escape route for dealers running from the police." In every neighborhood in this country where street-level drug dealing is going on, there are escape routes. In some places, the police chase dealers on a daily basis, and on a lot of days catch them. Sometimes, we post a couple of guys on the other side of the escape route to snatch up the dealers as they come running through. This is exciting and in some cases fun for both the cops and the spectators. On those occasions when the cops win, the dealers, who generally manage to ditch any drugs during the course of the pursuit, go to jail for a couple of hours or get a citation for jaywalking if they illegally run across a street. When the dealers win the race, they get the opportunity to brag to their buddies about having humiliated those fat-ass "donut-eatin'" cops once again. And so it goes.

Doesn't it make more sense to close the escape route, to "fix the fence?" It's not as exciting as a foot pursuit, but it works better. The beat cop didn't take a hammer and nails and fix the fence himself. He established a relationship with the property owner, explained the problem to him, and worked with him to get the fence fixed. Now that the dealers have lost their escape route, that location has lost its attractiveness as a drug-dealing spot.

In Avondale, another problem was a pay phone location. Pay phones are problems in lots of neighborhoods. They become magnets for loitering and drug dealing on corners. Can the beat cop yank out a pay phone when it is a source of problems? Although a lot of cops are tempted to take a sledge hammer and solve the problem, that is certainly not the recommended approach.

However, neighborhood councils and local business associations are effective in getting pay phones yanked. It starts when the beat cop works with them to solve the problem.

BEAT PROBLEMS ARE PEOPLE PROBLEMS

Problem solving depends on relationships. And creating and maintaining effective relationships is hard work. Cops who spend their time cruising the neighborhood with the car windows up, whose response on radio runs is to handle them as quickly as possible, do not do much in the way of developing relationships.

How then do we go about it? The average cop's day is filled with opportunities. Let's look back at our two hypothetical beat officers, Community Policing Pete and Reactive Jack.

Pete's day is built around people. Before he goes out in the field, he checks with the previous shift beat officer to catch up on beat activity since Pete's last tour. Next, he meets with the detective assigned to his beat. Some agencies have "Neighborhood or COP Officers" assigned to attend neighborhood council meetings and respond to neighborhood complaints. If this is the case in Pete's agency, there's another person with whom to touch base.

Pete's first run after roll call is a self-initiated visit to a troubled apartment building on his beat. Most every cop in the country can point to a large housing complex as a center for problems on his or her beat and, short of an air strike or a couple sticks of dynamite, most cops feel powerless to do much about the problems.

Oftentimes, the building's owners and/or managers seem unwilling or unable to do much about it. But, as Pete demonstrates, a successful partnership with a property owner can reap real dividends. Sometimes simple steps will go a long way. In other cases, the solutions require long-term effort. But the first step is establishing the relationship.

How do you do it? Locate the property owner. Explain the problems and, in many cases, the owner will take action to solve them. Sometimes the eviction of a troublesome tenant works wonders. Offer to keep the owner advised of problems that occur. Then follow up with a phone call giving details of the problem and the people involved. Most landlords are not fond of calls from the police, and they will take action. The key is to establish the relationship and work with the owner to stay on top of problems. Offer to help him with the problems. Security surveys and suggestions on physical changes to prevent crimes are easy things to do.

Our hypothetical beat cop Pete gets involved in tenant selection. There are lots of possibilities for constructively working with property owners, but most of the time the officer will need to take the initiative.

Pete's next run involves the common problem of kids on the corner. In most cities a gathering of people on the corner will generate a call to the police — disorderly teens, drug dealing and use, loud music, etc. These gatherings are sometimes harmless, just teens hanging out. Sometimes drug use and sales are involved. Often, area business people and residents are intimidated and want action from the police.

What options do beat cops have in this situation? Years ago the response was simple. The beat cop would pull up to a group on the corner and advise them that they were on his corner. His standard warning, somewhat cleaned up, went like this: "I'm going to drive around the block and when I get back anybody still on my corner will have his ass kicked."

Though that strategy is occasionally tempting, it has real drawbacks. The problem can be solved without a confrontation that is really a lose/lose situation for the beat cop.

For example. a beat officer assigned to one of the large public housing projects in Cincinnati began having after-school gatherings on a particular corner. Officer Bret Isaac would pull up to a group on the corner, get out of the car and start up a friendly conversation with kids in the group. The others would generally cross the street and regroup away from the officer. Isaac would cross the street and begin again.

"Isaac, you trippin'!" was generally the comment that signaled the kids were tired of the game and giving up. In usually less than ten minutes, all the corners were clear.

There's now research that supports Officer Isaac's experience. A study of police response to designated "hot spots" in Minneapolis found that increased police presence, including intervals at least ten minutes long, changed behavior on the corner, even after the police left. Simply driving through the area had no impact (Koper, 1998).

In many respects these "kids on the corner" are one form of the "broken windows" Kelling and Wilson (1982) described. Kelling and Wilson showed that the failure to fix a single broken window soon leads to other broken windows and physical deterioration. In a similar fashion, two kids on the corner become four, then eight; then there's a fight or a robbery or a drive-by. Beat cops, by consistently and effectively handling the problem early on, avoid the later incidents (not to mention the mountains of paperwork).

The research on crime "hot spots" had another interesting finding — hot spots that are not addressed tend to worsen and spread into the adjoining areas (Green, 1998).

Officer Isaac was able to handle the problem not only because he's a creative cop, but because of the relationships he had established with the people in the neighborhood. Most of those kids knew Isaac and he was able to approach them in a respectful and effective manner.

Our traditional officer Jack had opportunities to establish relationships to solve his beat problems. When he gets the alarm drop, his first reaction is to cuss the old lady who set it off again. Rather than sit on his rear end, a decent cop would get out of the patrol car and spend 15 minutes getting to know the woman and trying to understand what was happening.

Establishing a relationship with the lady might lead to Jack teaching her how to operate the alarm system. If that didn't work, a phone call to the alarm company requesting a verification call prior to dispatching a police car might solve the problem. But without taking a few minutes to help the lady to understand her problem, Jack ensures that this alarm run is one he will make again and again and again.

Later on, Jack gets a run to a bar for disorderly customers. Most beats have trouble bars, and they can mean real problems for cops. Bars generate fight runs, disorderly customers, loud noise complaints, felonious assaults, sex offenses, crowd problems, traffic problems, and drunk driving offenses (DUIs). Jack, like a lot of his cohorts, handles these a run at a time. Think about the possibilities when Jack begins to understand the bar as the source of his problems and applies some creativity to solving the "Bar Problem."

An early step would include meeting with the bar owner. Jack would go into this meeting with a lot of leverage. Bars typically operate with a license that is renewed annually. This license represents the owner's livelihood, and threats to contest the license, even nicely phrased, usually bring serious conversation about how to solve the problems.

If the bar owner is unable or unwilling to solve the problem, other measures might be available. One troubled bar in the College Hill area of Cincinnati was closed when the building's owner was brought into the picture. With each run, fight, etc., at the bar, an officer made a phone call to the building owner giving him details on the incident. The phone call was followed by a letter restating the problem and requesting cooperation. After six weeks and five letters, the landlord evicted the bar.

Officers in St. Petersburg, Florida, faced with an uncooperative bar owner, found a creative way to apply pressure. They contacted the bar owner's insurance company and mortgage company and described to them the problems around the bar. After including representatives from the insurance and mortgage companies in a meeting with the bar owner, the owner suddenly grew more cooperative (Winton, 2000).

Does this approach take some initiative, some additional time, and persistence? Absolutely. But think of the payoff in officer safety, reduced radio runs, and an improved climate for other area businesses. The additional effort by officers is clearly a good investment.

WORKING WITH CITIZEN GROUPS

Go to a community meeting? Most cops I know would rather go to a gun run. I've seen officers who are personable, funny, and at ease in the most difficult situations that cops face suddenly turn to jelly when they're asked to talk in front of a community group. They'll pass out a report, mumble a few words, and then head for the door.

Making presentations can be a lousy experience, but with a little preparation, training, and some practice, these meetings can be productive for beat cops and occasionally even enjoyable.

Most beats have organized groups of people. The most common are block watch groups, but community councils, business associations and civic groups also are found in most neighborhoods. Large apartment complexes may have tenant groups.

Most of these groups have some interest in working with the police. They want police officers to come to their meetings, if only for a few minutes. Most of all, they want to know "their" police officer on a personal basis.

Most people, even in crime-ridden neighborhoods, like the police. They like to talk to officers. They identify with police officers and generally respect the job officers do. People generally believe police work is a lot more exciting than the reality, and talking to an officer gives them a feeling of sharing in the excitement.

All these things work in favor of making community meetings as important to beat cops as making radio runs. There are a couple of simple goals for officers attending community meetings. One primary goal is information gathering. A cop at a community meeting is a little like a doctor at a cocktail party. People want the doctor to cure all their aches and pains and, in like fashion, everyone wants the cops to solve their neighborhood problems. So the cop who takes time to listen will hear about the junk cars, the people going in and out of certain addresses all day and night, and the kids left unattended while mama is out buying crack cocaine. Is a lot of it pointless complaining or petty neighborhood jealousies? Sure, some of it is. But think about the informants we use and the ratio of bullshit to good information. My experience is that cops can learn more about neighborhood drug problems in an active community meeting than they can from a lot of the nickel-and-dime hustlers we rush to make CIs (confidential informants).

A regular part of most community meetings is a crime report. Most people, including cops, have a distrust of statistics. They believe, as Mark Twain noted, "There are three types of lies — lies, damn lies, and statistics." Thus, a lot of cops will treat a crime report like a speed-reading exercise. It might go something like this:

> Yeah, well last month we had 22 burglaries, 33 B&Es, 12 robberies, 42 assaults, and 31 thefts from autos. We made 45 drug arrests and confiscated 5 grams of cocaine and 35 grams of marijuana. If nobody has any questions, I'll see you next month.

Crime statistics need to be presented with some background and explanation. I was at a community council meeting when a crime report very similar to the one above was presented. After the officer asked for questions, there was a minute of awkward silence. Finally, a gentleman in the front row raised his hand and asked "Officer, can you tell us what all that means?"

Well, what does it mean? Is crime going up, going down, staying about the same? Are these assaults and robberies street attacks, or are they teens victimizing each other at the high school?

The high crime rates of the early 1990s and the saturation coverage of crime stories by the media gave a lot of people the impression that crime was overwhelming the community and that it was unsafe to venture out of the house for fear of being attacked by predatory gangs of youths. George Kelling described the "terrible toll that fear has had on individuals and communities — abandonment of streets, neighborhoods, public transportation systems, and urban facilities" (Kelling, 1985). Cops in Austin, Texas saw fear of crime as so important that reducing fear of crime became a goal of their COP effort (Dietz, 1997). Officers can use the occasion of the crime report as a teaching opportunity to address fear of crime.

Here's an example. A few years ago, the day after the Super Bowl, the local newspaper reported that three women had been kidnapped and raped in the Cincinnati neighborhood of Northside. The story went on to say that the women had been driven around in a van, and after being sexually assaulted, they were thrown out onto the street naked. Anyone living in that neighborhood who read this story would have to be brain dead not to be seriously concerned. Rape and kidnap!! Damn serious business.

As is often the case, the real story was somewhat different. The women were exotic dancers who'd been hired for a Super Bowl party. It's probably safe to assume they weren't hired for their extensive knowledge of football. As the game progressed some bets were made, and as money changed hands the males determined that $50 was missing. Suspicion centered on the dancers, and one of the men performed what could delicately be described as an unauthorized body cavity search. Finding nothing, the women were loaded in a van, beer was poured on them and they were pushed out of the van a couple of miles away.

The 911 call came in as "naked women on the street," and the 30 initial responding officers were told a story of the women being forcibly snatched off the street and raped. Acting on information provided by the women, the suspects were located and detained as the investigation progressed.

The victims were transported to the hospital for treatment and a rape exam. The emergency room doctor who did the rape exam was somewhat surprised when she discovered a $50 bill.

When asked to explain the $50, the women recanted their story, refused to cooperate in the investigation, and the men involved were released.

Along with crime statistics, some information on crime prevention can be shared. A high percentage of burglaries occur with unlocked doors and windows. Laptop computers and cell phones lying in the open in cars are simply an invitation for a broken window and stolen property. There are some simple steps people can take can reduce their risk of being a crime victim. It's the job of a good beat cop to provide this information.

WORKING WITH OTHER AGENCIES

Police officers are the most visible symbol of government. They are generally also the only government officials to be available 24 hours a day, seven days a week. So it is not too surprising that people will complain to the police about all sorts of problems that a lot of cops simply dismiss as "not our problem." Those neighborhoods with high crime rates and high demand for police service also typically have lots of other problems — abandoned buildings, graffiti, litter, high rates of unemployment, lousy schools, and so on. Smart cops recognize that these problems are interrelated, and that effort to solve some of these problems will pay dividends in fewer crimes and calls for service.

Graffiti is a great example. While there are a few who view graffiti as "street art" and find something redeeming in it, the majority of people recognize it as a fungus in the neighborhood that needs to be stopped before it spreads. Much of it is gang-related.

Is graffiti a police problem? Left untended, like the broken window, it can become a police problem. In the late 1990s, there was a gang operating on the west side of Cincinnati. They called themselves GWD, for Gangsters with Drama. Nobody has ever been able to explain the genesis of that name, but it just didn't have the threatening ring of the gangs like the "Crips" or "Bloods" operating in other cities.

In 1997, a group of the dramatic gangsters spray-painted their initials in large letters — G W D — across a building in the neighborhood of Camp Washington. "The Camp" was not GWD territory, and Camp teens took exception to having GWD sprayed on a building in their turf. In retaliation they added to the GWD so that it read:

G	W	D
i	i	i
r	t	c
l	h	k
s		s

GWD was not amused. A few nights later, some GWD members unleashed a volley of shots in a drive-by at a group of Camp kids standing on a corner.

So graffiti can quickly become a police problem. What's the beat cop to do about it? In Cincinnati, the answer is a cooperative effort called Cincinnati Neighborhood Action Strategy or CNAS teams.

The origin of CNAS is that John Shirey, Cincinnati's City Manager, liked the community policing concept and decided to apply it to all city services. Other city departments, modeling on police, assigned their personnel to neighborhoods and charged them to work in concert with residents on neighborhood problems.

A neighborhood CNAS team typically consists of a representative from Fire, Health, Sewers, Buildings, Highway Maintenance, Sanitation and so on. The neighborhood beat officer is a member of the team and has an ongoing relationship with the workers from other departments. So if the beat cop has an abandoned building that is causing problems, he brings it to the attention of his partner in the Building Department.

CNAS sweeps have become an effective strategy to deal with drug houses. Most drug houses have a variety of violations; a coordinated, multi-department inspection will generally find enough building or health violations to either board the place up or bring so much attention to it that it loses its effectiveness for attracting drug customers.

CNAS teams vary in effectiveness from neighborhood to neighborhood. Some police officers have gotten very involved with their CNAS teams. Others probably think CNAS is a new soap opera. The difference is the relationship. Effective cops utilize the resources available to them, and CNAS gives them more tools to deal with the problems they encounter.

Beat cops with a problem building can call their counterpart on the CNAS team. They know and trust each other, and don't let the city bureaucracy get in the way of what needs to be done. These are the kind of relationships that pay dividends in better city services and more livable neighborhoods.

Police in Oakland, California, used a concept similar to CNAS to attack drug activity. City employees organized SMART (Specialized Multi-Agency Response Teams) groups that used civil violations of city fire, building, and public works codes in combination with law enforcement to successfully close down drug houses (Green, 1996).

ESTABLISHING RELATIONSHIPS: GETTING THE GLUE

Good beat cops establish good relationships with individuals and groups in their neighborhoods. How do they do it?

The August 8, 1999, edition of the *Cincinnati Enquirer* included a story about Tom Collins of Ludlow, a small town in northern Kentucky. "Everybody knows Tommy. He's the guy you see everywhere around town. He never met somebody whose mother, sister, brother or uncle he didn't already know... He's the town busybody. And the police chief."

The article quotes a fellow chief — "He's probably one of the best street policemen ever to hit northern Kentucky. The man's people skills are phenomenal. He treats people like people."

Chief Collins, commenting on a recent major arrest, said, "Some people say it's luck. But you make your own luck. You drive around. You stop and talk to people."

There is no magic formula for effective relationships. As Chief Collins has discovered, it takes hard work on a continuous basis.

We develop relationships in police work just like we do in every area of life. Treat people with respect. Work on listening skills. Follow through on commitments. Take time to understand problems before dashing off to solve them. Don't always be the expert. Make mistakes. Be humble. Try again.

But most of all, we have to work at it. Learn from mistakes. There will be plenty of those. Celebrate success and share the credit widely.

Chapter 4.
Problem Solving

The emphasis on solving problems is what separates our two styles of policing. Reactive Jack's day is dictated by the radio. Anyone in the community who picks up the phone and dials 911 has more control over Jack than his supervisor does. Jack's workday is not informed by any serious analysis of the problems on his beat. Instead, he runs willy-nilly where the radio calls lead. He handles the calls as quickly as possible, and in the time between radio runs he cruises about with little purpose while waiting for the next dispatch. For a lot of cops, that is the sum total of police work.

For beat officers tired of the merry-go-round of reactive policing, for cops looking for a more intelligent approach to police work, community policing emphasizing problem solving will be a godsend.

HOW DO WE SOLVE PROBLEMS?

There are a number of problem-solving models around. The most popular in police circles is the SARA process developed in Newport News, Virginia (Eck and Spelman, 1987). SARA stands for **S**canning, **A**nalysis, **R**esponse, and **A**ssessment.

Scanning involves identifying the problem. Analysis is an in-depth look at the problem, utilizing whatever statistics and information that can be gathered. Based on the Analysis, a Response is devised and implemented. Assessment is evaluating what happened as a result of the Response.

The SARA process provides a nice framework on which to hang problem-solving efforts. It is a circular process. The first step is understanding the problem (scanning and analysis). The second step is to take some action (response). Finally, we make a determination as to the effectiveness of the response (assessment). The assessment leads once again to scanning and analysis, since many neighborhood problems are not neatly or easily solved. It's a continuous process.

WHAT IS A BEAT "PROBLEM"?

Beat cops respond to a variety of radio runs in the course of a day's work. Maybe it's loud music, an assault, a traffic accident, a complaint about kids on the corner, drug complaints, a landlord-tenant dispute, or family trouble. What distinguishes these individual incidents from problems is a connection by location, complainant, time of day, suspect, or victims. If the beat officer is unable to connect an incident to others by any one of the factors above, it likely is an isolated incident and can be viewed as a single event.

Location is probably the single most obvious factor that ties together incidents. As noted earlier, research has found that 10% of addresses account for over 60% of police calls for service (Bieck et al., 1991). Most large cities are now using crime and calls-for-service data to identify "hot spots" that account for a high volume of both categories. Computerized dispatch systems linked with crime analysis can kick out reports sorting calls for service and crime by location.

This is the kind of thing most police officers don't really need a computer to tell them. Ask any beat cop where his problems are and he'll come up with a list in about five seconds. But even good beat cops often don't see the whole picture. Most cops, particularly those on fixed shifts, will see an eight-hour slice of beat life. A second shift officer could have problems at a certain corner where school kids are waiting for the bus home. On third shift or during the day, the corner could be quiet.

So time of day is also an important factor. Traffic problems, for instance, tend to cluster around morning and evening rush hours. A rash of daytime burglaries would be an example of a problem defined primarily by time.

Single offenders or groups of offenders could well be responsible for multiple crimes and police problems. In the same fashion, victim similarities, attacks on elderly women, or shootings of drug dealers could tie incidents together, defining them as problems.

It should also be noted that people in the community may have a very different perception of problems from the police. This was brought home to me in one of the first community meetings I attended. In the weeks prior to the meeting there had been a number of robberies of pizza delivery drivers. At that point, we had no suspects and very little positive to report. My concern was the possible hostile reaction when we reported our lack of progress.

There were about 75 people in attendance when the beat officer gave his crime report. He reviewed the pizza robberies in some detail, noting that we did not have suspects and not much to go on. He asked for questions, and I waited for the barrage.

An elderly man stood. "What I want to know is what are you doing about those kids leaving that chicken place and littering all over the street?"

A woman raised her hand. "Last week when I drove by the school some kids threw snowballs at my car."

Another man jumped up. "When are you going to do something about that guy across the street from me always working on his car in the middle of the night?"

Eight questions later, nobody had said a thing about the pizza robberies. Their major concerns were things that affected them personally — disorderly kids down the street, litter, loud noise complaints. These are exactly the type of quality of life issues that citizens complain about all over the country. Most cops find it hard to get too enthusiastic about working on snowball fights, loud noise complaints, or disorderly teens.

The inclination of most cops in the situation above would be to disown any responsibility for those problems. Call Litter Patrol. Talk to the schools about the kids. It's lack of recreation. We're too busy to respond to noise complaints! After all, we've got robbers to catch!

Nobody expects the police to give up responding to robberies so they can respond to loud noise complaints. But they do want their problems taken seriously, and the credibility of the officers is on the line when they offer themselves as community problem solvers.

Some of these things are not traditionally police problems. And some of them will take the cooperation of other community agencies. But by virtue of being the only 24/7 government service available, police officers will continue to receive these complaints, and the expectation of the community is that they take some action.

STEP ONE — SCANNING

What are the problems beat cops face? These problems run the whole gamut. Assaults, shoplifting, racial attacks, convenience store robberies, gangs, skateboarders, homeless people, graffiti, auto theft, truants, loud parties, drunk drivers, abandoned buildings, landlord-tenant disputes — and the list goes on and on. Beat cops interested in solving problems ask themselves, "Have I been here before? Can I expect to be here again? What's the pattern?"

Goldstein (1990) notes that police problems can be concentrated on certain beats (problem bar) or can be citywide (drunk driving). They can be relatively simple problems (thefts from autos in a certain parking lot) or complex (racial friction in a neighborhood). Some can be addressed by the beat officer, while others may require a high level of department commitment and obtaining cooperation from other agencies (drug dealing).

Officers can successfully address problems on their beats, but some problems are easier to solve than others. And some problems are not so much solved as they are managed. So in choosing problems to work on the beat officer would normally concentrate on those problems where he sees some chance of success.

Loud noise complaints and daytime burglaries are two problems that beat officers often grapple with. Look at how the SARA process might work for these two problems.

STEP TWO – ANALYSIS

The analysis step is simply the process of learning everything possible about the problem and how it occurs. If a loud noise complaint is the identified problem at a certain address, get some details. When is the problem occurring? Most agencies with a computer-aided dispatch (CAD) system can print out a history of runs to certain addresses.

- Are the complaints centered around a time of day or night? What other kind of runs have there been to that address? It's possible that loud noise complaints may be the tip-off to larger problems.

- Who is the complainant (or complainants)? Where are the complaints coming from? When one person calls repeatedly even though nearer neighbors have not complained, could it be indicative of the complainant using the police to push a personal grudge.

- What happens when officers respond? Get together with the those officers and get their read on the problem. What is the complaint location? Is it a business, a residence, an apartment building, a fraternity house, a drug house?

- What legal options do the officers have? Is there a local noise ordinance that could apply?

The analysis stage will lead to a greater understanding of the problem and possible solutions. Trying to solve the problem without doing a decent analysis is a sure recipe for failure.

There are two main problems to avoid in the analysis stage. The first is jumping to conclusions without really understanding the problem. The second is studying the problem to death, a method popular with a lot of government agencies. Paralysis by analysis is no better than jumping ahead with no analysis. Both lead to the same result.

The analysis should lead to a plan. It may be that the problem could be easily solved without an elaborate plan.

In his book, *Problem-Oriented Policing* (1990), Goldstein gives the example of a Philadelphia sergeant investigating repeated noise complaints about a certain bar. The sergeant learned that the complaints had all come from a single person living behind the bar. None of the other neighbors thought there was a problem, and the bar owner had cooperated in keeping the music down as well as turning off the jukebox after a certain hour. The complaints persisted.

The sergeant showed ingenuity by spending some time in the complaint's apartment and discovering that the vibrations from the jukebox were more the problem than the volume of the music. The sergeant suggested that the bar owner move the jukebox to another wall, and the problem was solved.

In Cincinnati, the neighborhood where the majority of noise complaints originates is the area surrounding the University of Cincinnati. Not content with mere house parties, some of the students prefer to block off streets for mini-Woodstocks, complete with lousy bands, drugs and extensive drunkenness. The usual police response to these parties is to warn on the first call. If a second complaint is received, the responding officer would shut down the party, sending everyone on their way. Occasionally, some open flask or disorderly conduct tickets would be written. In almost every case, that was the end of the story. Shut down the party and move onto the next radio run.

But after a particularly bad school year, when officers were rocked and bottled while breaking up parties, the beat cops involved and their bosses looked for a new approach.

Analysis of the problem revealed that most of the party animals involved were college students. The parties were almost always in rented houses or apartments, and officers looking at the problem decided to involve university officials and landlords.

University officials and university police agreed to work on the problem with beat officers. In fact, beat cops were surprised to discover that when students were involved in hosting these parties, the university was willing to take action against them.

The majority of the owners of the student housing were absentee landlords who either did not know or did not care what was occurring on their property.

STEP THREE — RESPONSE

After a lot of review, it was decided to take a somewhat different tack on the problem. Enforcement of the common misdemeanor violations (open flask, marijuana citations, etc.) at the parties was stepped up. On weekends, a small group of officers was detailed to respond to party complaints, violation ticket books at the ready. Often, beat officers were able to identify potentially troublesome parties even before citizen complaints came in, and the quick enforcement action generally put a damper on the festivities before they got out of hand.

On every loud party run around the university, responding officers identified the responsible person. It was never difficult to identify someone. If the party was on university property or was sponsored by a university organization (fraternity or sorority), or if the responsible person was a university student (or faculty member!), that was noted on the report for follow up.

At the officer's discretion, the party was either shut down, a warning was issued, or both. The warning was in written form, and it threatened both civil and criminal sanctions if officers were forced to respond again. The civil penalties were allowed under a city ordinance authorizing the city to bill party givers for the cost of police response to party complaints.

The loud-party reports were entered into a database. The owner of the property where the party had occurred was identified, and a phone call was made to the owner advising him or her of the problem.

In some cases, proactive measures were taken. Many of the larger parties were advertised on flyers posted around the university area. One enterprising officer discovered a section in the city's littering code that prohibited posting of flyers on telephone poles or placement on the windshields of cars. This section was used to discourage the posting of flyers around the community making the event-type parties more difficult to arrange.

Beat cops watched for the flyers and then contacted the prospective party giver. A visit from the police had an uncanny ability to smother the party spirit.

STEP FOUR – ASSESSMENT

As can be seen, the problem of loud parties is more complex than it first appears. Once we begin to analyze it, "loud parties" covers a multitude of problems. Each particular type of loud party might generate a different response. But, however the problem is defined and whatever strategies are chosen, the next issue is deciding whether or not we've been successful.

For the beat cop, success might be defined as not spending his Saturday nights breaking up parties. Other indicators would include fewer radio runs; fewer traffic accidents; less drunk driving; fewer assaults and fights; less litter; and, for the immediate neighbors, a good night's sleep!

Thorough assessment is as important as good analysis. Did our effort have any impact at all? Any and all sources of information should be utilized. Radio-run reports, citizen complaints, and crime statistics might all provide some indication as to the impact, if any, that our response generated.

In doing the assessment, also touch base with other officers involved. What is their perception of whether we had any impact?

Most of the concern about loud parties around the University of Cincinnati originated with citizens who complained to their local community council. Each Monday, the president of the community council would call the neighborhood officer to report on the "loud-party complaints" she had received. The neighborhood officer, in turn, provided information on the parties broken up, what citations were given, and how many parties would be billed under the city ordinance for the cost of the police response. This information exchange was an important part of the process, and officers were generally able to gauge their success on the party problem by noting the length of that Monday morning phone call.

The database created was also a useful tool for assessment. A six-month review of the calls and action taken found that contact with the landlord was an effective step in preventing further party problems at that location.

Remember, the SARA process is circular. Based on our assessment and analysis of the current state of the problem, we could declare victory (problem solved!) or, more likely, that the problem is somewhat improved. We then would modify our strategy. One result could be displacement of the problem to the next block. Or the positive effects of our problem solving might expand into nearby areas, which researchers call diffusion.

In some cases, assessment indicates that we haven't been successful. Time to try another alternative.

DAYTIME BURGLARIES AND SARA SCANNING

Burglars viewed the neighborhood of College Hill like lions watching a wounded gazelle. College Hill is a bedroom community with most of the houses empty during the day. Officers reviewing the crime statistics noted a sudden increase in burglaries.

But burglaries weren't the only problem plaguing College Hill. The neighborhood was also the site of Aiken High School, one of the largest public high schools in the area. The common complaint of the business community was that groups of young people were hanging around in the business district and roaming the neighborhood while they should be in school. A quick glance at the statistics showed the burglary increase coinciding with the start of the school year.

ANALYSIS

Most of the burglaries were within a mile of the school, and several were concentrated within blocks of each other. The burglars typically forced entry in a basement or side door shielded from street view. Jewelry, currency, CDs, and small appliances were the most common items taken. Crime scenes had not yielded usable fingerprints, leading investigators to believe the thieves were wearing gloves.

The truancy problem was more complex. The school had two special programs, Occupational Work Evaluation (OWE) and 8+. These programs complicated the truancy enforcement effort.

The OWE program was designed to provide students who were at risk of dropping out with a shortened school day combined with an afternoon work program. The students were released at 10:30 a.m. with the expectation they would either go to a job or look for work. In fact, they tended to cluster in the business district to hang out. Beat officers referred to OWE as the Out Walking Everywhere program.

The 8+ program was for 16-year-olds who hadn't yet passed the eighth grade. Rather than keep them in the junior highs, where they tended to be disruptive, the school district assigned them to high schools, where they were not quite official freshmen. The 8+ students were also released at 10:30.

In addition, there were a number of kids on the street every day who had been suspended or expelled from school. Officers were somewhat confused as to whether these kids had a legal right to be on the street during school hours.

The previous police response to the truancy problem consisted of periodic truancy sweeps in which hundreds of kids citywide would be picked up and taken to central locations to await picking up by parents. Each of these "round-ups" generated impressive numbers and TV news stories, but did not change the students' behavior. In fact, some officers believed truancy increased following a round-up as the kids figured they were safe for a least a few days.

RESPONSE

District officers met with the school resource officer and school officials to clarify the status of OWE and 8+ students. Two important decisions came out of those meetings. The school agreed that an OWE or 8+ pass was not a license to roam the streets. The students were supposed to have a definite job destination. They also agreed that OWE students loitering in the business district could be considered truant and taken back to school.

Around this same time city council passed a daytime curfew ordinance that specifically prohibited expelled or suspended students from being on the street during school hours.

One officer was assigned as coordinator of the truancy program. This officer worked with school and court officials to streamline the process of handling truancy offenders, making it easier for other officers to support the truancy effort.

At community meetings, citizens were encouraged to call in truancy complaints. The majority of the complaints came in during morning hours after rush hour traffic had subsided, and officers were generally available to respond to these complaints.

ASSESSMENT

In a matter of weeks, the streets were noticeably empty of kids during the school day. Citizen complaints about truants dropped off as the number of kids on the street declined.

A call about truants led to the arrest of juveniles responsible for 10 to 12 daytime burglaries. As beat cops had suspected, the large number of juveniles roaming the street had provided cover for the burglars. It turned out that the juvenile burglars were not from the local school but from a neighborhood on the other side of town. The burglaries were a gang initiation, and the juveniles were being transported to the College Hill neighborhood by older gang members.

The program was not a complete success because the truancy problem had to some extent been displaced to an adjoining jurisdiction. Unable to roam Cincinnati streets freely, the kids began gathering in a park just outside the city border, where they became the target of that police department's problem-solving efforts!

An interesting outcome of this problem solving was that the burglars were not, as all the beat cops had suspected, Aiken High School students. The burglars utilized the cover of the truants to blend into the community. Only when the truant problem was attacked was the burglary problem solved.

SUMMARY

Problem solving means a switch in thinking. The beat officer, rather than responding mindlessly to every radio run, applies some common sense to the problems on her beat. Instead of viewing everything as a separate incident, she begins to identify patterns in both crime and calls for service. Using the SARA process, she studies the problems, works with other people to understand the problem, and together with them, devises solutions. She tries it out and evaluates what happened. Based on the evaluation, she modifies the plan and tries again.

It's definitely not brain surgery! It works, but it takes commitment, some courage to try new approaches, and the support and help of people in the community.

Problem solving brings lots of benefits for the beat cop — fewer annoying radio calls, fewer community complaints, improved officer safety, and the satisfaction of actually accomplishing something helpful to the community.

Chapter 5.
A Word for the Bosses

BEAN COUNTERS AND PROBLEM SOLVERS

Community policing is an approach that each individual beat officer can apply to his day-to-day work. Will good bosses make it go easier? Without a doubt. Can lousy bosses cause problems? Again, without a doubt.

Supervisors, like police officers, run the gamut. First-level supervisors, sergeants and lieutenants can act to make a community policing effort by their officers a great success, or they can become obstructionists, another problem for the officer to work on.

Just like beat cops, a boss's effect depends on her philosophy, both of policing and supervision. A sergeant who thinks cops are wasting time at community meetings, who thinks police work begins and ends with answering radio runs, is not going to be too supportive of community policing or problem-solving efforts.

Another type of supervisor, one who is thankfully not seen too much anymore, is the boss with the mind-set of an accountant. This is the boss who carefully tabulates — how many tickets, how many radio runs, how many arrests, how many DUIs, how many cars towed. In her opinion, the numbers tell it all. Those cops who write lots of tickets are the best police officers. Quality is never an issue with her.

A variation on this supervisor is the one who thinks all the cops she supervises are trying to put something over on her. She'll prowl around, trying to catch her officers sleeping or drinking coffee somewhere. Her basic belief is cops are lazy slobs who will work only with a boss over their shoulder.

If you've got a boss who fits these descriptions, and we've all had them, good luck. They can make it very difficult.

SOLVING PROBLEMS VERSUS GENERATING NUMBERS

Bosses can assist their officers to be great beat cops by focusing first on doing the right things.

There is pressure in every police organization for numbers. Things happen and we react. A pedestrian gets killed: get out there and write some jaywalking tickets. A store owner complains about juveniles in front of his business: do some directed patrol. Complaints about drug problems: make some undercover buys and arrest some people.

Police agencies jump into action and we use numbers to justify what we do. But unless we do the right things, ask the right questions, the numbers don't tell the story.

I observed a new sergeant giving out "monthlies" to the beat guys on his shift. The monthly is a compilation of the officer's work, a total of tickets written, arrests made, cases closed, etc. After totaling the numbers, the sergeants and lieutenants would write comments on the back and give them to the officers.

Two beat cops I knew well got theirs together. "Outstanding, as always," the sergeant told the first guy, a cop who had a reputation for writing "hummers" — tickets for every minor violation he saw.

"Dan," the sergeant said to the second guy, "you apparently retired already. Why don't you put in your papers and make it official." It was obvious that Officer Dan wasn't much of a ticket writer.

But I knew Dan as an old timer with a lot of beat integrity. He didn't write a lot of tickets, but he took care of his beat and knew everybody on it. On slow afternoons, he'd pull his car off the side of the road at a spot where we had frequent crashes, put his flashlight on the dash so drivers thought he running radar, and would sit. He never wrote a lot of tickets. He did, however, prevent a lot of crashes. Compare this to the guy who wrote a lot of meaningless tickets to keep bosses happy. Who was doing the better job?

Here's another example. I got a call from a citizen. He told me, "On my way to work this morning, at 7:30 a.m., I got flagged down by some guys trying to sell drugs at McMicken and Vine Streets. Here I was, in my business suit and Honda — it just seems like it's out of control."

I think everybody would agree it was out of control. I called the lieutenant at our drug unit. "I just got a citizen complaint. This guy says dealers were trying to sell him drugs at 7:30 this morning at Vine and McMicken."

The lieutenant exploded. "Jesus Christ! In the last six months," (I heard the sounds of paper shuffling), "we made over 200 arrests at that corner." We both got quiet as the reality of the problem set in. Judging by the numbers, our efforts at that corner had been tremendous — lots of arrests, and, no doubt, a serious amount of drugs confiscated. But the problem persisted. It was apparent that our response, arresting a lot of people, wasn't working.

Some wag said that the definition of insanity is to continue the same behavior, always expecting different results — a good description of the police effort at that location. The problem-solving approach says let's be accountable for actually having an impact on the problem. It defines success differently. Success is not just making arrests or confiscating drugs. Success is when the citizen drives by and there are no dealers out there trying to sell him drugs. Sometimes arrests can accomplish that. When they don't, it's time to more closely analyze the problem and try to develop a response that does.

CHANGING THE RULES

If bosses want cops who are going to be problem solvers they need to set the proper expectations for officer behavior. Supervising problem solving is more complicated than the bean counting method. If supervisors are not going to judge performance by the numbers, how should they do it?

If officers are going to solve problems on their beat, the first step to understand what the problems are

— in the SARA model, scanning. We ask our beat cop — "You're running Westwood. What do you think are the problems on that beat?"

If this is a new approach for a supervisor and/or the officer, don't be surprised if the initial response is a variation of "I don't know." Most cops have never thought about their daily beat work as response to community problems. They go into service at the beginning of their shift, go where the dispatcher tells them, and they take care of whatever comes up in their eight-hour tour.

Given a few minutes to think about it, most beat cops can eloquently describe the problems on their beat. It's the apartment building, a pay phone, a video arcade, a family of thugs, a biker bar, and the whole raft of social problems that cops have to respond to.

If the officer is unable to identify problems, the supervisor can help him. The first step is identifying people who know what the problems are and establishing relationships with them. This can be a sticking point because cops usually do not see it in their job description to "establish relationships."

The better question is likely something along the line of — "Who knows what the problems are in your neighborhood?" There may be people inside the department who can help to answer that question. Larger departments have crime analysis units. Good supervisors not only make sure that beat cops get copies of appropriate reports, but they also spend some time with the officers discussing and interpreting the report.

Other beat cops are a great source of information. Too often, beat cops on different shifts see each other in and out the door at shift change and never get a chance to share information. Communication across specialized units is also a problem. Investigators, neighborhood officers, gang-unit officers, drug investigators, school resource officers and the variety of others tend to work within their own units and can quickly lose touch with patrol officers. It takes an ongoing effort to keep these relationships alive and useful.

There are people in the community who have useful information. School principals, ministers, business people, recreation workers, and social service workers are all great sources of information. This information is only available if the relationship has been established.

Good supervision would include helping the officer identify these sources of information, encouraging ongoing contact with them, and then following up to make sure it happens.

As emphasized in Chapter 3, community meetings are a great source of information. Most cops are not enthusiastic about attending community meetings. Supervisors can help by pointing out that attendance at a community meeting is just as important as making a radio run. Cops are also more open to community meetings if supervisors help them see it as an information gathering exercise, no different from meeting with an informant. Often, the results will be better.

As beat cops move through the problem-solving cycle, there will be numerous opportunities for supervisors to assist. Constant reinforcement that problem solving is the way to better policing is crucial. It means freeing officers from routine duties so they can pursue problem solving. It means making arrangements to cover the radio so officers can take the time for problem solving. It means helping cops identify and use community resources to solve problems. It means going to bat for the officers when others question problem-solving strategies.

Most of all, it means judging and holding supervisors and officers accountable for results, not numbers.

LONE RANGERS AND BAT TEAMS

Most police work is done by officers working alone. Groups of officers might respond to serious incidents and two-officer cars may be assigned to high crime areas, but the day-to-day grunt work of a beat cop is carried out by the individual officer.

While imaginative beat cops can do a lot of problem solving on an individual basis, sometimes problem-solving teams can be more effective. Formation and leadership of such teams is generally a supervisory function.

Cincinnati's Police District Five consists of four beats. To facilitate problem solving, supervisors organized a BAT Team, or Beat Action Team, for each beat. The BAT teams consist of a beat officer from each shift, the detective assigned to that beat, and the neighborhood officer assigned to that beat. Each BAT team is headed up by one of the district's lieutenants.

The BAT teams generally meet each month. At the meeting, the monthly crime report is reviewed as well as a radio-run report. The radio-run report is a listing of every address that had had three or more radio runs in the previous 30 days. The report shows the date and time of each run, the complaint code (disorderly, alarm, noise, man with a gun, etc.) and the run disposition (sent on way, report, arrest, etc.) This report is an excellent tool for problem solving.

The lieutenant begins the meeting by reviewing the radio-run report. The obvious question is "What's going on there?" Sometimes the problems are simple.

Multiple alarms at an address on Cherry Street — the resident is an elderly woman beginning to have mental problems. She lives alone and sets off the alarm when she hears noises or gets scared. What do we do?

The neighborhood officer is assigned to contact the woman's relatives to make them aware of the problem. She also visits the woman's neighbors, who agree to check on her more frequently. Finally, a social service agency is contacted for an in-home evaluation.

Next, a number of runs to a convenience store for disorderly customers — the calls seem to clustered after midnight. The third shift beat officer laughs: "The store just hired a new clerk to work third shift and she's scared. Every time somebody looks at her sideways, she calls the police." The first shift officer volunteers to talk to the store manager, who eventually transfers the clerk to another location where she feels less intimidated. Problem solved.

As the meeting goes on, pictures of suspects in recent crimes are circulated. Information is shared about new people in the neighborhood, as well as the status of problem people on the beat. Complaints from the community are reviewed and strategy developed. Different people are assigned for follow up at specific locations, and will report progress at the next meeting.

Organizing problem-solving groups like BAT teams accomplishes two major things. First, it creates the expectation that beat cops can solve problems on the beat and that it is, in fact, their responsibility to do so. By having bosses in leadership roles, it legitimizes problem solving as officer activity.

Second, BAT teams open communication among officers on different shifts and across specialized units. The increased level of awareness of beat problems and steps underway to solve them makes better beat cops of all the officers participating.

Other Cincinnati districts have adopted the BAT team model. In some places, they're called NAT, or Neighborhood Action Team, or NIP, Neighborhood Improvement Teams. Whatever the name, the principles are the same.

Some cops have taken the problem-solving group idea to its natural next step — citizen participation. For example, as part of Chicago's Alternative Policing Strategy, beat meetings have included residents in order to ensure that the police are responsive to problems identified by residents (Dubois, 1995).

Money Talks and...

Captain Phyllis Caskey of Cincinnati Police is a commander who not only talked the talk but walked the walk as well. When her district was allocated money to support overtime for additional patrol, she took the road less traveled. Rather than simply pay officers to add to the regular patrol force, she dedicated the funds to support problem solving. And she did it in a way that forced bosses to get involved.

Each district lieutenant was allocated funds to support problem solving on one of the district's beats. This made BAT meetings more lively. Now the BAT teams had some bucks to support their ideas to address beat problems. And as might be expected, the BAT teams and the cops involved in them responded. One beat decided that a foot patrol team assigned to the neighborhood business district would address complaints about drug dealers and customers loitering in the area. Another team used their funds to support additional officers to handle problems stemming from disorderly crowds leaving high school football and basketball games.

Allocating funds to support problem solving means going beyond loose talk about community policing to real implementation. It's walking the walk.

SOME DO'S AND DON'TS

A lot of bosses, like some of the cops they supervise, don't see any need to change the way they do business. They have a view of police work that does not include working with people in the community. In their opinion, problem solving is the work of people at United Way or a job for social workers, not cops. There is little anyone can do to change these types of attitudes.

Good supervisors can make all the difference in effective policing. The Police Executive Research Forum (PERF) has developed the following list of supervisory actions that would assist cops in their problem-solving efforts. Some examples from the list are:

- Allows officers freedom to experiment with new approaches.
- Insists on good, accurate analysis of problems.

- Grants flexibility in work schedules.
- Protects officers from pressures within the department to revert to traditional methods.
- Knows what problems officers are working on and whether the problems are real.
- Coaches officers through the problem-solving process, gives advice, helps them manage their time, and helps them develop work-plans.
- Gives credit to officers and lets others know about their good work.
- Coordinates efforts across shifts, beats, and outside units and agencies.
- Identifies emerging problems by monitoring calls for service, crime patterns and community concerns.
- Provides officers with examples of good problem solving so they know generally what is expected.
- Provides more positive reinforcement for good work than negative for bad work.

In contrast, a study of supervisors during implementation of Chicago's Alternative Policing Strategy program identified some supervisory actions that got in the way of officer problem solving (Geller and Swanger, 1995):

- Bean-counting on performance evaluations.
- "Bad mouthing" community policing during roll calls.
- Micromanaging officers' efforts.
- Favoritism to certain officers.
- Ruling through rules, fear, and intimidation.

There are benefits to the bosses who take the leap and support their cops in community policing. A study of community policing in Houston found fewer citizen complaints against officers in those areas where community policing had been implemented. Researchers credited the emphasis on community partnerships with reducing tension between police and citizens (Kessler, 1999).

Another study in Edmonton, Canada, found that the community-policing program not only effectively reduced repeat radio runs and increased citizen satisfaction, but increased the job satisfaction of the officers involved as well (Hornick, 1991).

Effectively supervising community policing is a more difficult task than overseeing traditional policing.

If you are interested in working with your cops as a team member and coach, if you are able to look beyond bean-counting, and if you believe the police work that you do can truly make a difference in your community, then you are ready to begin.

Chapter 6.
It Can Be Done

KIDS KILLING KIDS

In 1987, Boston had 22 youth (age 24 and younger) homicide victims. By 1990, youth homicides in Boston had increased over 200%; and from 1991 to 1995 youth homicides in Boston averaged 43 per year (Brito and Allan, 1999). Faced with escalating violence that threatened to overwhelm authorities, Boston police formed a working group to study the problem.

In analyzing the problem, several key factors were discovered. Most of the violence was gang-related and concentrated in a few neighborhoods, and a small number of gang members in these neighborhoods were responsible for the bulk of the violence. The kids involved were well known to authorities. A study of the homicide victims found that 75% had been involved in the juvenile justice system, many of them multiple times. A study of the offenders found a similar pattern. Over a quarter of the offenders had previously been locked up in state juvenile institutions and a similar percentage of offenders were on probation at the time of the offense (Brito and Allan, 1999).

The same analysis also showed that gun trafficking was an important component of the problem. Acquisition of guns by the involved teens appeared to stem largely from fear for personal safety.

The original working group grew to include local juvenile probation officials, who had launched an innovative street probation project, Operation Night Light, that focused on working closely with Boston police as well as local social services. The Night Light project was targeted at the same group of kids that the working group had identified as at high risk for youth homicide.

The group decided to include federal authorities: the Bureau of Alcohol, Tobacco, and Firearms (ATF), the Drug Enforcement Administration (DEA) and others. Working closely with federal authorities as well as with local juvenile probation officers, a comprehensive response to the youth homicide problem was developed. That response became known as the "Cease Fire" strategy.

The "Cease Fire" strategy had two components. First was an attack by the Boston police on gun trafficking. In cooperation with the ATF, police concentrated on tracing the origin of confiscated firearms and aggressively prosecuting offenders. Information on gun trafficking was developed through systematic debriefing of gang members arrested, and this effort resulted in a large increase in trafficking prosecutions.

The second component was an organized effort to target law enforcement resources against individual gangs, to create a deterrent to gang-related violence. Boston police spread the word that violence by gang members would bring down the whole weight of the authorities on that gang's operations. Concentrated effort by the authorities could make a gang's existence very miserable. Disrupting street drug sales, active enforcement of criminal trespass and other minor violations, active warrant enforcement, and cooperative effort with probation officers to enforce probation conditions were just some of the tools authorities could use to seriously disrupt gang operations.

Gang officers, probation officers, and neighborhood street activists enlisted to help in the effort spread word of the police threat. The police even organized gang forums where the strategy was outlined directly to gang members.

Cops knew that their threat would surely be challenged and that failure to make good on their threat would mean business as usual for the gangs and a sure continuation of the violence cycle.

In 1996, after gang violence directly related to the Dorchester Vamp Hill Kings, Boston police and their allies decided to make the Vamp Hill Kings their first target. The orchestrated police action broke the gang, and the news that the Kings' violent activity had brought about their own demise was loudly broadcast, both in the city's media and through the informal gang network.

The action against the Vamp Hill Kings bolstered the Cease Fire project's credibility with the gangs. In effect, the message was, "We said it, we meant it, and here's proof of that: here's what they did, here's what we did, here's how you steer clear" (Brito and Allan, 1999).

In the summer of 1996, the Intervale Posse was chosen as the next target for the Cease Fire project. Long known as one of Boston's toughest crack-dealing gangs, the dismantling of the Intervale Posse by Cease Fire was a watershed event.

A study by Harvard researchers (Brito and Allan, 1999) working with the project found youth homicide rates down 70% from the years just prior to Cease Fire. Street surveys determined that Cease Fire had broken the previous cycle of violence among the gangs. Citizen surveys documented that both adults and youths in Boston felt safer in their neighborhoods and less concerned with the threat of violence.

Since Boston's success, the Cease Fire strategy has been used in a number of other cities. Operation Cease Fire received the 1998 Herman Goldstein Award, recognizing exemplary problem-solving projects (Brito and Allan, 1999).

RESEARCH RESULTS

Cops across the country, from Boston to Seattle, from Baltimore to San Francisco, are working to solve crime and disorder problems. The book *Fixing Broken Windows*, describes how the police, in coordination with other public officials and community groups, are successfully tackling problems like homelessness, aggressive panhandling, and graffiti that are threatening the social fabric of big cities (Kelling and Coles, 1996). There are a tremendous number of community policing efforts that have been studied by researchers, and their success is well documented.

For example, in 1989, Tampa police had identified and targeted 141 active drug-dealing locations. The QUAD (Quick Uniform Attack on Drugs) program focused on suppression of drug dealing through active enforcement, order maintenance and community involvement. Patrol operation priorities included: improving citizen involvement and communication; involving cops from every unit of the police department; and working closely with the media. Within a few months, only nine of the original locations were still active (Kennedy, 1993).

Newport News, Virginia, was the location of the first well-studied application of the SARA problem-solving model by patrol officers. Newport News police identified the New Briarfield Apartment complex as a location with a high rate of burglaries. The complex was run down, and a survey by officers found numerous unsanitary and unsafe conditions. Working with the complex manager and other city agencies, many of the deterioration problems were addressed, and the burglary rate fell by 35% (Eck and Spelman, 1987).

In the downtown area of Newport News, officers identified robberies as a problem. By targeting frequent offenders, robberies in the studied area were reduced by 40% (Eck and Spelman, 1987).

In New Jersey, Jersey City cops decided to target locations where most of their violent crimes occurred. Patrol officers worked to address the "broken windows" problems at these locations, and focused the uniform patrol effort on street disorder problems like public drinking and loitering. Researchers found "noteworthy reductions" in every violent crime category. The researchers also noted that the crime reductions were accomplished without displacing the problems to other areas (Braga et al., 1999).

Some cops have used a community policing approach to attack a different sort of problem. Chico, a community of about 45,000 people in Northern California, is home to two colleges, a state university and a community college. These institutions add another 23,000 people to the community during the school year.

In 1990, Halloween became the occasion for full-scale rioting in Chico when crowds of drinking students and young people took over the streets, causing property damage, fights and assaults that overwhelmed the small police department.

As Halloween of 1991 approached, Chico cops developed a strategy to prevent a recurrence of the previous year's disturbances. The centerpiece of the plan was the involvement of numerous volunteers, who were outfitted in orange traffic vests. Working in teams with officers and supervisors, the volunteers presented a friendly but formidable presence that provided a sense of security and a deterrent to disorderly behavior (Aeilts, 1994).

The examples cited are only a small cross-section of the tremendous variety of community policing efforts going on all across the country. Criminal justice research is rich with examples of police departments, working with their communities, having clear success in solving crime and disorder problems.

But the bulk of community policing is occurring around the country on individual beats in places large and small. Thousands of cops, with varying levels of organizational support, flying by the seats of their pants, are applying common sense and determination to solve the problems they confront daily. Few of these efforts will ever be the subject of criminal justice research publications. For the most part, the efforts lack the research design and methodology that could document statistical success. Nonetheless, these efforts show that individual cops, by approaching their work in a fashion different from the detached law enforcement officer of the past, can be effective in solving problems on their beats.

Following are some additional examples.

Reaching Out to Kids in Winton Terrace

By 1994, Winton Terrace had become a policing nightmare. The Terrace is one of Cincinnati's largest public housing projects. Always one of Cincinnati's more dangerous neighborhoods, conditions got real ugly after two drug dealers killed each other in a street gunfight.

When the media responded the next day, crowds throwing rocks and bottles chased them from the neighborhood. Utility crews got the same treatment. Then a few local politicians showed up with news crews for their regular "photo-op"; the politicos were jostled by angry crowds and quickly retreated.

Police were faring no better. After a police car had its brake lines cut while the officers were handling a family fight, two cars were sent on every run in the Terrace — one to handle the call and the second to guard the police vehicle of the first officers.

Officers Cal Mathis and Bret Isaac worked as a two-officer beat car covering the Terrace on second shift. Isaac and Mathis were experienced, aggressive beat cops who made a lot of arrests, and in the eyes of the cops working with them "were knocking them stiff in the Terrace." Both had received death threats, and Isaac had shots fired at him as part of a planned ambush by local gang members. Both had been part of numerous police strategies to regain control of the neighborhood — drug sweeps and buy busts, and intensified patrol. Both were frustrated and looking for another way.

In the mid-1990s, Sega computer games were a popular item in the country and in the Terrace as well. Isaac and Mathis decided to use the popular video game system as a tool to develop some positive relationships with the kids in the Terrace. Using donated games as prizes, the two beat cops organized a Sega tournament with the kids, competing under police supervision. The number of kids taking part the first year was small. But word got around, and the Sega tournament took on a life of its own. It grew to become a major event in the community, attracting crowds of spectators as well as participants.

Building on this success, the two decided to organize a basketball league. Using the local recreation center as a base, Mathis and Isaac created a youth basketball league modeled on the National Basketball Association (NBA). Team names and uniforms copied the NBA, and prior to the league opening each year a draft of players was held, with participants assigned to teams based on their position in the draft. The teams still play once each week and compete with an intensity that puts many NBA players to shame.

During the process of organizing these events, Isaac and Mathis developed relationships with resident leaders, school personnel, the managers of the complex, and the wide variety of social service people working in the Terrace. These relationships opened the doors for lots of creative strategies for neighborhood improvement.

Each week, Mathis and Isaac began to review the radio runs to the Terrace. Those residents who generated police activity were "invited" to a sit down with the two cops in the presence of Ms. Jean, the Project Manager. If there was an identifiable problem, help was offered. The carrot was always accompanied by the stick. Unless the problem, whatever it was, was quickly remedied, eviction would follow. Ms. Jean was a no-nonsense person, and those who tested her quickly found themselves looking for another place to live.

Over the next few years, crime and disorder in the Terrace fell dramatically. How much of the decline could be credited to the efforts of beat cops Isaac and Mathis? It's difficult to say. A federal grant provided additional foot patrol in the neighborhood, and many people think the additional police presence was an important factor. Yet this same grant provided additional presence in other housing projects that did not experience similar declines.

In addition, the director of Cincinnati Metropolitan Housing Authority (CMHA) was an advocate of Crime Prevention through Environmental Design. As a result, CMHA invested a lot of funds in landscaping and fencing, much of the funding targeted at reducing criminal opportunities.

In sum, the reduction of crime and disorder in the Terrace was likely due to a variety of factors. However, it would be difficult to find anyone familiar with the changes in Winton Terrace who did not give a lot of credit to the work of beat cops Bret Isaac and Cal Mathis.

Both Mathis and Isaac have moved on in their careers. Isaac was promoted to sergeant in 1998, and Cal Mathis is now a detective assigned to Winton Terrace. Mathis continues to utilize the relationships he developed as a beat cop, and rarely does anything happen in the Terrace without Detective Mathis knowing about it.

The Sega Tournament and the Terrace NBA Basketball League are still going strong.

Ashwood Apartments

The Ashwood apartment complex is no different from thousands of others around the country. Built as low-income housing, the apartments consist of 12 large buildings, each housing 15 to 20 separate units. Although privately owned, the complex is subsidized as a U.S. Department of Housing and Urban Development project.

Over the years and through various owners, the complex deteriorated. The parking lot of the complex was dotted with junk autos. Windows and doors in the buildings were frequently broken. Tenants complained about poor maintenance, and police runs to the complex were common.

New ownership in 1996 brought some changes. The new owner, a Chicago businessman, quickly became frustrated when his efforts to upgrade and improve the complex failed.

The owner thought that expanded police presence at the complex would help. He began to hire off-duty officers to work at the complex, first for eight hours each week and, when that proved ineffective, for 16 hours per week. The off-duty officers patrolled the grounds, responded to radio runs that originated in the complex, and made note of problems, broken lights, and the like for follow-up by maintenance workers.

Crime and disorder problems persisted. The owner's breaking point was reached with a string of violent crimes in the complex, culminating in the shooting of a resident. Following the shooting, the owner flew to Cincinnati and met with Sergeant Don Schroder.

Sgt. Schroder began to look into the problems at Ashwood. Most of the officers working Ashwood considered it pretty much of a lost cause. There was no expectation that police presence would do anything but prevent crimes while the off-duty officers were working. The officers put in their hours, continued the routine of patrol and response, and blamed the ongoing problems on crime-prone residents.

After meeting the owner and hearing his frustration, Sgt. Schroder decided to apply some problem-solving principles at the Ashwood complex.

Sgt. Schroder began by taking steps to develop some relationships between the residents and the cops. First, he limited the number of officers working the detail to himself and one other officer. The officer chosen, Terry Smith, was a community-minded officer who accepted Schroder's challenge to approach the problems at Ashwood in a different fashion.

Next, a large meeting of the residents to discuss problems at the complex was held. The violence in the complex had scared most of the residents and they were hungry for some changes. A large crowd attended that first meeting.

Despite the violence, the primary complaints of the residents were junk autos in the lot, poor lighting, and the general physical deterioration of the complex. Sgt. Schroder pledged to work with the owner to solve the problems.

Junk autos was the first problem to be attacked, and Sgt. Schroder knew the residents would judge them by their success in getting the autos removed from the lot. After laying the groundwork, Sgt. Schroder and Officer Smith spent the next few days in the parking lot very visibly checking auto registrations against the list of tenants. Twenty-four hours later the tow trucks showed up and the lot was quickly free of junk autos.

Two other immediate physical steps were taken — repaving the parking lot and upgrading the lighting around both the parking lot and the complex buildings. These changes, made with the financial support of the owner, identified the officers as people who could get things done.

By limiting the number of officers working at the complex, Schroder and Smith quickly became known by the residents as the Ashwood Apartment cops. As they began to get to know the residents, Schroder and Smith looked for those with leadership potential.

There had been several previous failed attempts to develop a residents' council at Ashwood. Few residents would attend meetings and the meetings themselves were poorly run, often degenerating into bitch sessions that accomplished little. The most obvious problem was identifying leaders and keeping them involved and motivated. To assist with motivation of potential leaders, Schroder developed a unique incentive.

A special parking space was identified for the Resident Council president and the space was chosen for its proximity to the resident's door. The space was identified by sign as reserved for the Resident Council president, and this seemingly small but concrete recognition was important for the president and the other residents.

One of the first things the newly elected Resident Council organized was a community fair and cookout. The fair, held on a Saturday afternoon, had a variety of games and enjoyable activities for both adults and kids. At Schroder and Smith's request, many of the other officers who were assigned to the Ashwood area attended. At the cookout, residents interacted comfortably with each other and the police in a remarkable contrast to the suspicious and fearful behavior that had characterized the community only a few short months before.

With Schroder's help, the Resident Council continued to work on improvements in the complex. Kids with good report cards were given coupons for free pizza, a computer room was established to teach computer skills to both adults and children, and the council became involved in assisting and welcoming new residents.

The impact of these efforts on crime and disorder at the Ashwood apartments has not been formally studied. Further, it's unknown whether any of the effects survived Sgt. Schroder's transfer to Internal Investigations a few months later. It is clear that Sgt. Schroder and Officer Smith, by putting community policing principles in practice at Ashwood apartments, interrupted the downward spiral at the complex.

What they did was not complicated. They established working relationships with the owner and with the residents. By limiting the officers on the detail to himself and Officer Smith, Sgt. Schroder helped to identify the two of them as cops with names and faces, people committed to working with residents to improve the complex. And by taking action to solve problems, to address resident concerns, Sgt. Schroder and Officer Smith gained a credibility that all the talk in the world would not have accomplished.

Organizing Across Units

When a new gameroom opened up in Northside, neighbors were justifiably concerned. The area already had gang problems, a history of racial problems, and an active street drug market. Despite the gameroom owner's protestations that he only wanted a nice place for the kids to hang out, both residents and police foresaw problems.

One of the owner's first steps was to paint a large mural that totally covered the side of the building, an area twice the size of a typical billboard. The mural was a montage of rap stars in vivid colors. Actual painting of the mural took about a week, and it is difficult to overstate how important this mural became. Each day crowds of curious residents gathered to watch the work in progress, speculate about the motives of the owner, and complain about the worsening conditions in the neighborhood.

The finished mural added to the community uproar as all the rap stars portrayed on the wall were black. After loud complaints about the "lack of diversity" on the mural, the owner took action to soothe feelings. Over a weekend, the mural sprouted a large Elvis Presley squeezed between Tupac Shakur and Puff Daddy.

But the Elvis fans in the neighborhood weren't mollified, and within a couple of weeks of the gameroom's opening, there were fights, complaints of drug dealing and increased reports of disorderly kids on the corner. Gang tensions focused on the gameroom and culminated in a drive-by shooting within a month of the gameroom's opening.

The gameroom and its problems generated a lot of police activity. Neighborhood Officer Joe Hill was working with community groups concerned about the gameroom. At Officer Hill's request, the District Five Criminal Apprehension Team (CAT) started surveillance on the gameroom. The CAT Team was a tactical unit that did a lot of drug work.

Residents had also complained to the Cincinnati Police Division's Gang Unit about gang activity at the gameroom, and Operation Street Corner (a street drug enforcement unit) had begun an investigation of the location due to numerous complaints. Beat cars were also responding to calls about problems at the gameroom and fielding resident complaints.

To try to coordinate the activities, Hill and his supervisor organized a meeting of all the various units that were responding in one fashion or another to the gameroom. After sharing information, the units formulated a loose plan that at least guaranteed they wouldn't be tripping over each other in their efforts to solve the problem.

Within three weeks, a CI (confidential informant) working jointly with the CAT team and Operation Street Corner, purchased cocaine at the gameroom. A search warrant was served a few hours later, and a quantity of drugs, drug paraphernalia, and money was confiscated. The building owner, who had formerly been a staunch supporter of the gameroom (no doubt an Elvis fan), closed it down and the problems disappeared.

BUILDING RELATIONSHIPS AND SOLVING PROBLEMS

If we look at each of these examples, we see some things in common. In Winton Terrace, Officers Mathis and Isaac did not sit down and in a systematic way identify the major problems on their beat. But they knew instinctively that they were involved in a struggle for the hearts and minds of the kids in that neighborhood.

In coming up with the Sega tournament, they may well have chosen a solution without really analyzing problems in a fashion recommended by some of my academic friends. But in organizing that youth activity they set into motion some very positive things. When people working for the recreation center, people managing the housing project and community leaders recognized that Isaac and Mathis, these two beat cops, were committed to helping the neighborhood; these people then rallied to assist the officers. The simple gesture of organizing something for the neighborhood kids had marked Isaac and Mathis as leaders and made them the focal point of efforts to improve the community. Once Isaac and Mathis had established a high level of credibility, the relationships leading to problem solving came more easily.

At the Ashwood apartments, Sgt. Schroder took a somewhat different tack. The owner of the complex, certainly an important person in any problem solving, initiated a relationship and offered resources. Schroder took two important steps to build on this foundation. First, he limited the police officers directly involved to himself and Terry Smith. Second, he sought resident input in identifying problems at the complex. When residents identified junk autos as a problem, that became an opportunity for Schroder and Smith to establish credibility. By solving the junk auto problem, Schroder and Smith identified themselves as serious people who could be trusted to follow through with resident concerns.

The gameroom problem in Northside was somewhat different. Here was a situation identified both by residents and police as a problem even before the place opened. But the initial police response was disorganized and marked by poor communication. To effectively solve the problem, someone had to take the lead and bring the various players together. It is something that too seldom happens in policing. It is also a good case example of a situation where supervisors need to take the lead to organize problem-solving efforts that include various police units.

The type of activity found in these three examples is going on all across the country. Individual officers and sometimes their bosses see things that need to be done. They work with the people on their beats and they go ahead and do it.

In almost every case, these officers are acting outside the norm of policing. They may get recognition from their peers or supervisors for going "above and beyond," and that is exactly the problem.

Community policing says problem solving should be the norm. Every officer can approach his beat with an attitude that his job is not simply to answer the radio but to solve problems. When that happens, officers like Mathis, Isaac, and Schroder will no longer be the exceptions but the rule. Beat cops and the neighborhoods they work in will be the winners.

Chapter 7.
Getting Started...

BEAT COPS

You're convinced. You've just been assigned to a new beat and you believe community policing and problem solving is the way to do your job more effectively. But how exactly should you get started?

The first step is information gathering. It's your beat, and you will quickly learn a great deal about the people who live there and the problems they face. Begin to put it to paper. What is the beat profile? How many people live there? What do you know about the population? Are they primarily from one ethnic group or is it a mixed neighborhood? Is the neighborhood primarily composed of young people, couples with children, or single mothers? Are there a lot of kids in the neighborhood?

What about the residential pattern? Are there a lot of apartment buildings or primarily single-family homes? Are most residents owners or renters? Is the area primarily residential, business, or a mix? How would you describe the beat economically? Are people primarily middle class, working class, upper class, or a mix?

What are the important institutions on the beat? Are there churches, schools, hospitals, businesses? Who are the community leaders? What community groups exist?

Do you have a beat map? What are the main vehicle routes through the beat? Is there a lot of pedestrian traffic? Are there parks, parking lots, or major employers? How about fast food restaurants, convenience stores, bars? What is the overall physical condition of the beat? Are there a lot of "broken windows"-type problems?

Answering these questions will give you a profile of the population and the physical layout of your beat. The next step is developing a general understanding of the crime and disorder problems on your beat.

Has crime been stable, increasing, or decreasing? Do you have a lot of street crime? Drug markets? Gang activity? Problem bars? What are the problem locations on your beat — hot spots — the places you find yourself responding to again and again? Does the crime you respond to have any pattern — location, similar victims, same offenders? A review of crime reports or any radio-run reports your agency generates will be helpful.

Any and all information you can find about the beat will be helpful. But developing a good beat profile is not entirely a desk job. The best way of answering some of these questions is to get out on your beat and learn it. Drive around your beat with your eyes wide open. Then get out of the car and do some foot patrol. You will see some things on foot that you won't from a patrol car.

As police officers, we're trained observers. Look at your beat with cop's eyes and then write the information down. Once you've done the preliminary work, it's time to begin the partnership building.

Who are the leaders of the community? What organized groups exist? Are there business associations, community councils, ministerial groups? If there are schools, are there student and parent groups? Are there service clubs in the area — Jaycees, Lions' Clubs, Rotary Clubs, Kiwanis, Chamber of Commerce?

At some point, any or all of these groups and the individuals in them might be of help to you. But the first step is getting to know them.

COMMUNITY SURVEYS

Willie Sutton was once asked why he robbed banks. He looked at the questioner in disbelief and retorted, "That's where the money is!"

In like fashion, if you want to know what people in the community think, ask them. Community surveys are an excellent tool for identifying what people in your beat believe are problems. Surveys can range from long carefully structured questionnaires to informal questioning and conversation.

Surveying people in the community really has a dual purpose for beat cops. First, we're learning what people think are problems. But just as importantly, in the process of discussing community problems we're getting to know people in the neighborhood. By asking them their concerns, we demonstrate that the police are interested in what citizens think, and we begin to develop the partnerships, the relationships, that will make us better beat cops.

Some of the issues that typical surveys cover are crime, disorder-type problems (abandoned buildings, junk autos, etc.), fear of crime, perception of the police, and the willingness of citizens to work with police in block-watch or other programs.

Doing surveys is not much like traditional police work. But there are important benefits. Surveys alert beat cops to problem areas and community issues that may be simmering below the surface. The fact of the survey itself is concrete evidence of police involvement in the community, and, if done on a regular basis, the surveys will provide some feedback on the relative success of police problem-solving initiatives (Marenin, 1989).

SUPERVISOR'S EYE ON THE BALL

There are specific steps that a field supervisor, sergeant or lieutenant can take to facilitate his officers' transition from traditional policing to community policing. Most of all, the boss has to keep his eye on the ball. In community policing, the ball is problem solving and a "results" orientation. If the supervisor concentrates on the right things, his subordinates will follow. Some specific examples of keeping an eye on the ball include:

- *Make solving beat problems the bottom line of* discussions *with your officers.* Instead of praising one of your cops for writing a large number of tickets, focus on results. At what location are tickets being written? Is there a problem there? Is writing citations a good way to solve the problem?

- *Provide your officers with the best information available and help them interpret it.* With the advent of computerized crime analysis, most departments can generate sophisticated reports on crime and disorder problems by beat. Provide these reports to the beat cops and review them together. These reports will help to highlight beat problems as well as provide the basis for assessing the relative success of your problem-solving efforts.

- *Reward the right things.* When one of our officers makes a great arrest or closes a difficult case, you would write him up for a chief's commendation, and rightfully so. Success in problem solving is less dramatic and more likely to involve a long-term effort. But these efforts are just as deserving of commendation, and you send a powerful message when public recognition is granted to the officer or officers involved.

- *Protect your officers from petty sniping.* There will be people both in and outside of the organization who will be taking potshots at cops involved in community policing. Like hecklers at a baseball game, they cannot be allowed to distract the batter.

- *Organize problem-solving groups.* Organizing groups like the Beat Action Teams described in chapter 5 is a supervisory job. Putting together problem-solving groups sends a powerful message that problem solving is in fact legitimate activity and that beat cops have a role to play in working on neighborhood problems.

- *Arrange for training.* Training in presentation skills, doing community surveys, report writing, crime analysis, and working in groups can help beat cops be more effective. There are Community Policing Institutes now operating around the country that will provide this training at no cost. Local universities may also want to become involved.

There are other steps to make community policing more effective that are beyond the authority of first-line supervisors. As a part of an organization-wide move to community policing, redrawing beat boundaries, implementing differential police response strategies, flattening the organizational structure, implementation of substations, civilianizing positions, and writing grants for new officers are all things that management could consider. In the 1990s, Charles Ramsey, Chief of Police in Washington D.C., completed a major overhaul of his department's structure with the goal of facilitating community policing.

Ramsey cut his teeth on community policing as a deputy superintendent with the Chicago Police Department. His D.C. reorganization focused around beat cops and first-line supervisors by emphasizing accountability to the community, enhancing management of beat-level operations, and initiating a geographically-based structure from the top to the bottom of the organization (Ramsey, 2000).

WHAT'S IN IT FOR ME?

You may be thinking that you've got enough headaches without taking on the chore of working with your people to solve beat problems. Further, it's obvious that supervision in this style of policing is more difficult than in traditional policing. And despite the evidence, you're still skeptical.

Skepticism is a healthy attribute for successful supervisors. Good police supervisors cannot afford to be running from one faddish idea to the next. Policing is serious business, and most supervisors are reluctant to change direction without hard evidence that something works.

The good news is that there is evidence that community policing not only works with community problems but will directly benefit police supervisors as well.

For example, take the issue of job satisfaction. There is persuasive research evidence that beat cops involved in community policing are more satisfied with their work than other officers. A study of cops involved in Chicago's community-policing effort found them more satisfied with their jobs, more optimistic, and more positive about their relationships with citizens (Lurigio and Skogan, 1998). A study of New York cops found similar results (McElroy et al., 1990).

The findings of increased job satisfaction also include supervisors. A study of patrol sergeants in Austin, Texas, found patrol supervisors in a new community-policing effort supporting job changes that allowed them to work with teams, having the freedom to choose projects, and working with citizens (Bradstreet, 1997).

FOR FURTHER INFORMATION

If you are interested in community policing, there are a couple of books to put on your must-read list. First on almost everyone's list is *Community Policing: How to Get Started* (1984) by Robert Trojanowicz and Bonnie Bucqueroux (Anderson Publishing). Trojanowicz is generally considered the father of COP and this book is a great introduction to community policing philosophy and practice.

The U.S. Department of Justice has published a guidebook for law enforcement agencies interested in doing community surveys. If your department plans on using surveys as a major part of its community-policing effort, a review of this publication may be helpful (Weisel, 1999).

For an introduction to problem solving, read *Problem Oriented Policing* by Herman Goldstein (McGraw-Hill). For an excellent case study of the SARA problem-solving process in action read *Problem Solving: Problem-Oriented Policing in Newport News* by John Eck and William Spelman (Police Executive Research Forum or PERF).

The best publication I've seen for a realistic treatment of problem solving is the *Problem Solving Quarterly* published by PERF.[1] Written in a newsletter format, each issue contains case studies of cops doing problem solving in their neighborhoods. Just as an example, the 2000 Winter/Spring issue had articles written by: a police officer in Charlotte-Mecklenburg, describing his effort to reduce robberies at a large apartment complex; a Pensacola officer applying problem solving to street drug dealing; and a Joliet cop trying to reduce radio runs to calls for service at rental properties in his city. The articles detail successful strategies for dealing with the problems that cops all over the country are struggling with.

TRAINING

In the mid-1990s, the federal government funded Community Policing Institutes around the country. There are currently about 30 such institutes established around the country. These institutes are charged with providing free training for police officers. They typically provide training modules on community policing, problem solving, ethics, running a Citizen's Police Academy, and a variety of other topics.

For example, the Regional Community Policing Institute (RCPI) located in Cincinnati is one of these federally funded institutes. RCPI provides training throughout Ohio, Indiana, and Kentucky. Trainers have even gone to major cities, like Dayton and Columbus, and provided round-the-clock training to include second and third shift officers.

Most of the Community Policing Institutes have websites. Search the web for a site near you.

For futher information on Community Policing Institutes, contact:

> U.S. Department of Justice
> Office of Community Oriented Policing Services
> 1100 Vermont Ave., N.W.
> Washington, D.C. 20530
> Phone: (202) 514-2058

CRIMINAL JUSTICE RESEARCHERS

University faculty and cops have historically had a suspicious view of each other. Both suffer from stereotypical views of the other and too often believe they have little in common. But, in fact, relationships between police and university people have tremendous positive potential for both parties.

For example, a few personal contacts and discussion on police issues between individual officers and University of Cincinnati criminal justice researchers have blossomed into a formal relationship allowing for university evaluation of various police initiatives. The police get objective reviews of the effectiveness of some of their projects, and faculty members get to apply their expertise to real-world problems.

THE INTERNET

No discussion of resources would be complete without a mention of the Internet. There are websites specifically directed at police problem solving. One example is POPNET, sponsored by the Police Executive Research Forum (PERF). POPNET is an online service with a database of police problem-solving projects from around the country.

Information on the web is growing every day. Enter "community policing" in your search engine and you'll find police websites, training programs, books and discussion groups.

FINALLY...

Being a great beat cop is tough. As a friend of mine says, "It's not rocket science. It's more difficult." Solving the toughest of human problems is hard work. It takes patience, intelligence, courage and a heavy dose of common sense. Good cops need the sensitivity of a therapist, the faith of a bishop, a novelist's imagination, and the guts of a warrior. But cops around the country are succeeding at it everyday.

You can be one of them.

References

Aeilts, A. (1994). "The Citizen Volunteer: Walking a Beat in Chico." *Police Chief* (November):39-41.

Bieck, W., W. Spelman and T. Sweeney (1991). "The Patrol Function." In: *Local Government Police Management.* Washington, DC: International City Management Association.

Bradstreet, R. (1997). "Policing: The Patrol Sergeant's Perspective." *Journal of Police and Criminal Psychology* 12(1):1-6.

Braga, A., D. Weisburd and E. Waring (1999). "Problem-Oriented Policing in Violent Crime Places: A Randomized Controlled Experiment." *Criminology* 37(3):541-580.

Brito, C. and T. Allan (1999). *Problem Oriented Policing.* Washington, DC: Police Executive Research Forum.

Dietz, S. (1997). "Evaluating Community Policing: Quality Police Service and Fear of Crime." *Policing: An International Journal of Police Strategy and Management* 20(1):83-100.

Dubois, J. (1995). "District Advisory Committees." *Community Policing Project Papers*. Chicago, IL: Northwestern University, Center for Urban Affairs and Policy Research.

Dukes, D. and P. Kratcoski (1995). *Issues in Community Policing*. Cincinnati, OH: Anderson Publishing.

Eck, J. and W. Spelman (1987). *Problem-Oriented Policing in Newport News*. Washington, DC: Police Executive Research Forum.

Geller, W. and G. Swanger (1995). In: *Managing Innovation in Policing*. Washington, DC: Police Executive Research Forum.

Green, L. (1996). "Policing Places with Drug Problems." In: *Drugs, Health, and Social Policy Series* (vol. 2). Thousand Oaks, CA: Sage.

—— (1998). "Cleaning up Drug Hot Spots in Oakland, California: The Displacement and Diffusion Effects." *Justice Quarterly* 12(1):737-754.

Goldstein, H. (1990). *Problem Oriented Policing*. New York, NY: McGraw-Hill.

Hornick, J. (1991). "An Impact Evaluation of the Edmonton Neighbourhood Foot Patrol Program." *Canadian Journal of Program Evaluation* 6(1):47-70.

Kelling, G. and C. Coles (1996). *Fixing Broken Windows*. New York, NY: Simon and Schuster.

—— T. Pate, D. Dieckman and C. Brown (1974). *The Kansas City Preventive Patrol Experiment: A Technical Report*. Washington, DC: Police Foundation.

—— and J. Stewart (1991). "The Evolution of Contemporary Policing." In: *Local Government Police Management*. Washington, DC: International City Management Association.

Kennedy, D. (1993). *Closing the Market: Controlling the Drug Trade in Tampa, Florida*. Washington, DC: U.S. National Institute of Justice.

Kessler, D. (1999). "The Effects of Community Policing on Complaints Against Officers." *Journal of Quantitative Criminology* 15(3):333-372.

Koper, C. (1998). "Just Enough Police Presence: Reducing Crime and Disorderly Behavior by Optimizing Patrol Time in Crime Hot Spots." *Justice Quarterly* 12(4):649-672.

Lurigio, A. and W. Skogan (1998). "Community Policing in Chicago: Bringing Officers on Board." *Police Quarterly* 1(1):1-25.

Marenin, O. (1989). "The Utility of Community Needs Surveys in Community Policing." *Police Studies* 12(2):73-81.

McElroy, J., C. Cosgrove and S. Sadd (1990). *CPOP: The Research – An Evaluative Study of the New York City Community Patrol Officer Program*. New York, NY: Vera Institute of Justice.

Ramsey, C. (2000). "Organization Change: Preparing a Police Department for Community Policing in the 21st Century." *Police Chief* (March):16-25.

Trojanowicz, R. and B. Bucqueroux (1994). *Community Policing: How to Get Started*. Cincinnati, OH: Anderson Publishing Company.

Winton, K. (2000). "Ft. Meyers, Florida: A Case Study in Successful Community Policing." *The Law Enforcement Trainer* 15(2):10-13.

Weisel, D. (1999). *Conducting Community Surveys: A Practical Guide for Law Enforcement Agencies*. Washington, DC: U.S. Bureau of Justice Statistics.

NOTES

1. PERF has recently combined *Problem Solving Quarterly* with another PERF publication, *Subject to Debate*.